ALSO BY DEB BROWN…

Lessons From the Rocking Chair:
Timeless Stories for Teaching Character

LESSONS
FROM THE

Beach Chair

NATURE'S WISDOM
FOR TEACHING CHARACTER

Deb Austin Brown

LESSONS FROM THE

Beach Chair

NATURE'S WISDOM
FOR TEACHING CHARACTER

For information, contact:
CHARACTER DEVELOPMENT PUBLISHING
P.O. Box 9211
Chapel Hill NC 27515-9211
(919) 967-2110, fax (919) 967-2139
E-mail: respect96@aol.com
www.CharacterEducation.com

Cover design by Sandy Nordman Pogue—Odyssey Design
Text design by Sandy Nordman Pogue—Odyssey Design
Text editing by Ginny Turner

ISBN 1-892056-05-4 $9.95

Quantity Purchases

Companies, schools, professional groups, clubs and other organizations may quality for special terms when ordering quantities of this title. For ordering information, contact the Customer Service Department of Character Development Publishing at the numbers listed above.

FOR MOM AND TOM...
who loved the sea.

"LISTEN TO THE EARTH!"

—John Travolta as "Michael"
…in the motion picture
of the same name

TABLE OF CONTENTS

And so it is that I've come to love the sea. Books, music, poetry, movies, travel brochures, and magazines—they have all called me there. I spent much of my childhood searching out the sea. I would save anything that helped me remember. Pictures of the seashore, old fishing docks, sailboats, and lighthouses. Pictures of the sea oats, sand dunes, and shore birds…and especially the water crashing on the rocks. My memory is like a scrapbook of nature. My own travels over the years have added to that collection.

Life constantly changes, but never the sea. It has been the same since the beginning of time. Her lessons are timeless, too. The same ageless wisdom of the sea lives on—from generation to generation. Her message is for all who come to look…and to learn.

It is my hope that the lessons found within the pages of this book will help you in your travels. Nature's lessons on character are among her *best* wisdom. I claim these lessons for all of us who have ever loved the sea. It is my hope that this collection of beach chair wisdom warms your heart, and touches your life… in wonderful ways!

Deb

foreword

FOREWORD

In her first book, *Lessons From the Rocking Chair*, Deb Brown shared with us the great lessons in living passed down from her great-grandmother. Deb has applied them to her own life and passed them along to her readers in short, lively, thoughtful, and touching essays. It's no wonder that so many people bought the book in its first year of publication. It's one of those easy reads that we can open to any page and get a great boost for the spirit. It's also become one of those special gifts that friends give to friends.

Well, you're in for a treat because Deb has done it again! Only this time she shares more of her own wisdom. It comes to us from years of learning, teaching, and experiencing all that life offers. She'll make you laugh, and maybe cry, but most of all, she'll make you think about what's good, important, and meaningful in life.

In one lesson Deb tells us to share our joy. She practices what she preaches, so you'll find her own joy of living on every page. The magic is that she does it so authentically. It's a message straight from her heart, and it's bound to touch your heart as well. In another lesson Deb shares what she learned from one of her greatest losses: "Love life, and live it to the full! Cherish each and every day." And near the end she reminds us to constantly renew ourselves with the words: "We keep living…we keep learning." This is the essence of the book.

Lessons from the Beach Chair is a treasure—simple words of wisdom from a loving mother, a creative and caring teacher, a dynamic speaker, and a wonderful friend. Read it, live it, and pass it on to those you love.

Dr. Hal Urban
Author, *Life's Greatest Lessons*

introduction

INTRODUCTION

Messages are all around us. The messengers in life are disguised as parents, teachers, sages, and friends. They are disguised as historians, poets, philosophers, and counselors. They have learned and are willing to share life lessons from the human experience. Those of us who want to learn life's greatest lessons seek them out. We read, study, research, and ask in a quest that becomes a life journey toward wisdom. In my own journey, I have traveled each of those paths. I have also sought out the brilliant thinkers of our time. I have worn out their doorsteps and have listened to their words. They have taught me so much.

I have also looked around me. I have listened to the earth and have learned her lessons. Nature has her message. The sunrise at the beach, the wooded paths through the West Virginia mountains, and the sunset over Lake Norman—all have been my teachers. Perhaps the greatest character lessons for me were learned at the shore. I feel called to share the wisdom.

This book is an invitation to spend some time with me, walking the beach. To spend some time getting to know the sea. To spend some time getting in touch with the earth. Like the proverbial message in a bottle that washes ashore, this book has a message for its readers. The message is simply this: Look for the good in life. It's all around us.

I believe that life was meant to be good—and that we were meant to contribute to that goodness. I believe we were meant to spend the interlude between birth and death growing in knowledge and growing in character. Nature is the best teacher of this timeless wisdom. If only we would heed her message. This book is a collection of the wonderful life lessons learned at the hand of that master teacher—Mother Nature. We can learn from her that living a life of character is the only true way to a happy life. It seems so simple. But life's decisions are not always simple. Many times in my life, I've ignored these lessons and been lost at sea. Fortunately, someone has come along to throw me a life preserver. There has always been a lesson tucked inside.

So take your shoes off, pull up a beach chair in the sand, and sit with me by the sea. Let's visit one of the most beautiful places in the world…the beach. It is truly one of God's greatest gifts! And, if we pay attention to the lessons that can be learned from life-by-the-sea, we will learn nature's wisdom about the real goodness in life. The message in my bottle is the greatest message of all—the character message. It's the one message that will make the world a better place, one person at a time. It has the power to change your life! By learning and living the character message, you will find the goodness and happiness we all seek in life. So, pop the cork…and read on. The messages washed onshore during my beach visits can help you find the goodness that will enrich your life. Each of these lessons has certainly enriched mine.

Nature's wisdom is all around us. The first step is listening. Then comes learning …and taking the messages to heart. But the real joy comes from living these lessons day to day. So, listen, learn…and live! Listen to the earth, and look for the joy. I trust that you will find it!

Deb Austin Brown

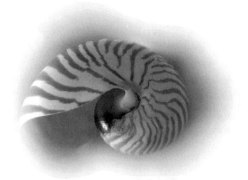

Listen To The Earth!

The beach is a wonderful place to get in touch with the earth. In fact, the beach is a wonderful place to get in touch with life! It's where land and water come together in a spectacular way. Millions of people flock to the seashore each year to take in the sights. And, with each visit, they are revitalized in wonderful ways.

In the 1996 motion picture "Michael," John Travolta played the part of a fun-loving angel sent to earth on a matchmaking mission. Michael had a good heart and a lighthearted spirit. With his wisdom and unique perspective on life, he reminds us of the important lessons we can learn from living. In my favorite scene, Michael is sitting on a farm tractor looking out over green Illinois farmlands just as dawn is breaking. You can almost hear the wake-up call of the rooster and can almost feel the fresh morning breezes. All of nature awakens as Michael takes in a deep breath, and smiles…"Listen to the earth!" You can truly feel his joy!

Listening to the earth is pure pleasure. When I'm at the seashore, I tune in and really listen. The sounds are incredible! Who could resist the pounding of the surf, the squawk of the seagulls, and the whistling of the wind through the palm trees? I love to walk the beach. But, like Michael, I love to sit and just take in the wonder of it all! The sights and sounds of the seashore are among God's best miracles.

Each morning I head for the beach just before sunrise. I sit alone on the cool morning sand and wait for the spectacular arrival of daybreak. There's nothing like it when the sun begins peeking out of the Atlantic Ocean! A smile spreads across my face as my endorphins kick into high gear! I sit, stilled with wonder, as the sun rises out of the ocean and takes its place in the coastal sky. I love to watch the sun come up…and, with tears in my eyes, I always applaud afterwards. It's such an incredible event, I wonder why everyone else isn't out there, too. The sun deserves a standing ovation from all of us.

Perhaps the reason Michael had such a keen appreciation for the earth was because he had been away from it for a long time. It made me wonder how many of us are really listening to the earth…and appreciating it. It's a life-lesson worth learning from an angel. Hopefully it won't take a heaven-sent messenger to get all of us to tune in to the lessons of the earth. All we really need to do is listen. Every once in a while, the earth will give us a little glimpse of heaven—but we've got to be paying attention.

In December of last year, I took my first winter trip to the seashore. It was a spur-of-the-moment decision. I packed up shorts, long-sleeved shirts, a sweater, my tennis shoes, and my beach journal—and headed south. During the nine-hour trip, I thought ahead to all of the miles of sandy beach that waited for me down the road. It was fun just anticipating it! My car wound through the mountains of West Virginia and Virginia. The weather was clear and cool. Dropping out of the mountains, I crossed the border into North Carolina. My smile began growing. By evening I was feeling the fresh ocean breezes of the South Carolina coast, and my smile was in full bloom!

The next days were warm and sunny. I counted my blessings by name: sand, water, pelicans, sun, sailboats, ocean breezes, palmetto trees, moon, and stars…plus the gift of time just to enjoy it all. Each day I would head from my family's beach house to the more remote Pawleys Island to write. Beach journal and pen in hand, I'd take my familiar spot in a beach chair near the sea oats and sand dunes. And then, I would watch and listen.

Watch and listen. Listen and watch…and write. It doesn't get any better than that! I noted observations; I wrote down my thoughts and feelings. I recorded any inspirational bit of wisdom that came to me with the roll of the waves and the wisp of the wind. Whether I would sit for a few minutes or an entire afternoon, there was always a lesson to be learned. Each glimpse of heaven is direct from nature, with a lesson that lingers long after the sand is dusted from my feet. The more visits to the beach I get under my belt, the more beach chair wisdom I've packed away in my suitcase before heading for home.

That cloudy evening was the last of 1996. I walked the empty beach hoping to glimpse the sunset. I climbed the dunes; I took lots of pictures. I smiled with delight at the passing of fifty-four brown pelicans flying in formation. It was then that I saw it—a single break in the dark clouds of evening. The year's last ray of sunshine shone down on the sand where shorebirds were crouched at the water's edge. It was a glimpse of heaven—and I had noticed! Michael would have been proud.

I carried off my beach chair that evening with a life-lesson written inside my journal and tucked away in my heart. I had listened to the earth, and it was good. In fact, it was…heavenly!

Beach Chair Wisdom:
There are many lessons we can learn from the earth, if we just pay attention. Life offers us little glimpses of heaven. So, learn a lesson from one angel-of-a-teacher: Listen to the earth!

Find Yourself At Sea!

I've been asked if I take the beach for granted. I've thought about it a lot before I answered, and the answer is no, I don't take the beach for granted. I live almost five hundred miles away, and I make the trip for a coastal visit at least four or five times a year. With each visit, I fall in love with the beach all over again! I marvel at each sunrise, each flock of pelicans, and each reassuring change of tide. But I've always wondered if the residents of the shore take life-by-the-sea for granted. My friend Mike has lived at the beach for thirteen years. I know that he loves his life there, but Mike often gets so busy with his work and his family that a walk on the beach and fishing from the pier get squeezed out of the picture. Mike just saw his first beach sunrise this past year. I couldn't help but wonder…what took him so long?

Three summers ago, I packed up my most necessary belongings and headed south. For July and August, I lived at the seashore. I'll have to say, it was just as incredible as it sounds! With my sons, Aaron and Ben, out of school and on their own, it was my first chance to leave the nest. I packed up shorts and tennis shoes, lots of books and writing supplies, my CDs and beach journals all into the trunk of my high-mileage sports car…and was off for the summer adventure I had dreamed of.

My car seemed to make the five-hundred-mile trip on pure adrenaline! I unpacked my belongings and settled in to a solitary existence in my family's beach house in a Carolina town. It was a different kind of summer. My family and friends were four states away. I saw no familiar faces at the post office or grocery store and no friends waving to me from passing cars. There were no former students giving out hugs at baseball and soccer fields. My telephone was mostly silent. A knock at my door was a rare event. I really was on my own. Cut off from hometown family and friends, I spent my summer building beyond the horizon of home.

Most days the routine was the same. I'd watch the ocean sunrise and take a fast-paced four-mile walk on the beach, then shower and read until midday. I'd have lunch with my two beachtown friends, then go to Mike's office and kick around ideas about our writing projects. I'd take a leisurely afternoon beach walk and eat dinner alone at a small waterside restaurant, then drag my beach chair through the sand to a familiar spot so I could sit, watch, listen, and write my way to the sunset. Watching the sky grow dark each evening was the icing on the coastal cake! If it sounds like an incredibly wonderful day, then I've done a good job telling the story.

There is something deeply rewarding about living at the beach. Visiting the seashore is grand, but living there is the real treasure. I didn't have to worry about tourist concerns, like trying to cram all the fun into the boundaries of a week or two. No pressures… no worries. All I had to do was just settle in and enjoy coastal life. And, it was profoundly enjoyable.

That summer, I missed my family and friends. I made new friends, though…friends of the earth: sunshine, ocean breezes, sailboats on the horizon, the full moon rising out of the ocean, and star-filled nights. Like hometown friends, they always made me smile. The brown pelican became my favorite seaside friend. Seeing a flock of pelicans fly by in formation brought me pure joy. I learned to take comfort in their company. It's hard to explain, but whenever the pelicans were around, I never felt lonely.

It was a wonderful summer of solitude, a chance to get in touch with…me. In the hustle and bustle of hometown life, I often put me on the back burner. My life gets filled with going to work, paying bills, washing the car, and mowing the yard. Finding time for deep thoughts and self-reflection is always a challenge. I do take a little time out each day for me, but this summer I was doing it right.

I spent a lot of time reading, and writing…and thinking. I spent time getting to know myself all over again. I found myself…at sea! Getting in touch with you is never a bad way to spend your day. Just getting the pressure of day-to-day living off of my back was a real treat. Relaxation became a new word in my own personal vocabulary. I was able to adjust my attitude, think through my life, and set some new goals for myself. In just eight short weeks, I had treated myself to a refresher course on life…and, a refresher course on Deb.

At the end of the summer, I packed up and returned home with mixed emotions to the beautiful mountains of West Virginia, which I also love. On the five hundred miles of northbound highway many thoughts tumbled around my mind. I reviewed all the things that had happened during my beachtown summer—all the things I had learned. Upon my return, many hometown friends asked me if I had come to take the beach for granted. Again, I thought before I answered. And, again my answer was no. Whether it's a short stay or an extended visit, I appreciate each morning sunrise, each roll of the waves, and each salty breeze. Each pelican that flies by is counted among my blessings of the day. It's such a wonderful thing to spend time at the seashore, I couldn't possibly take any of it for granted. Being at the beach is the best way I know to celebrate being me!

Beach Chair Wisdom:
Take time out of your busy
life...for you. Find yourself
at sea! A trip to the seashore,
to the mountains, or to the
solitude of a hometown park
can be the retreat that you're
needing in life. Don't take
you for granted. Get in touch
with a real wonder of
nature. Get in touch
with...you!

Build Beyond The Horizon Of Home!

At long last…here I sit, my beach chair parked in the sand. For more than a month I have come to live by the sea. I'm taking these weeks of summer to stretch myself beyond usual hometown boundaries.

Today at the beach, a sand crab keeps me company. He gently teases me into a game of hide-and-seek. As he dances sideways in the sand, he leaves broomlike tracks around my chair. He is clever company for me, alone on this beach Tuesday. The waves roll in as the morning sunlight dances on the water. Even God's own natural diamonds cannot measure up to the sparkle of this sunlight on the sea. Although breathtakingly beautiful, it curiously commands little attention from the tanned inhabitants of the shore.

Across the waters, off in the distance…the pelicans fly. In perfect V formation they come, gliding effortlessly along. Taking time out for a morning snack, they dive straight down into the blue depths below. They are, by far, my favorite seaside creature. Airplanes pass overhead carrying banners of invitation to southern tourist attractions. A sailboat appears on the horizon—its yellow and white sails pointing upward to God's sky. The breeze today is slight…too lazy to cool the warm skin of August sun seekers.

White-capped waves roll and pound the shore—their crashing sound is soothing background music to this seaside resident. Children dance with delight as they frolic along the water's edge. The toddlers whose toes touch the surf, perhaps for the very first time—marvel at this world, ever so new. They eagerly squat to pick a shell from the sand, a new treasure. A dog runs to catch a ball thrown in sandy play. He tiptoes through the surf to please his seaside master. Eagerly, he returns for another chase…and a pat of approval.

Lifeguard whistles sound in the distance, carefully guiding those too far out, safely back to shore. Colorful beach umbrellas dot the strand, and I watch their owners oil themselves against the sun, walk in the surf, and stroll up and down the beach. Bare bellies, bronze bellies, and beach-burned bellies—take their places walking towards the pier, as the familiar faces from home pace the well-traveled walkways of my mind. The universal principle applies: people are the same across this hometown world of ours.

The blues today are many. Even Crayola has not mastered the reproduction of this many shades. Blues, whites, and tans fill up the horizon this August beach morning. As I sit, looking out over the ocean, I think of all that I have learned here. Of how much I have grown.

After spending the summer here, this beach is different now…it's more familiar, more a part of me. My life is different, too. I cannot walk the sands ahead without chasing thoughts of home along the shoreline of my mind. My heart lives on in both towns… hometown and beachtown alike. When heading north, it's always an emotional tug on my heartstrings to drive away from the shore. And when I am at home in the mountains, my heart will ache for this beach life, which is a real part of me.

I am the architect and builder of my own vision to happiness. I have already built a home and life many miles away to the north. This is the summer of building beyond the horizon of home. This time I'm building on familiar beachtown sands. I've seen the ocean at this beach, and come to know it through each of my senses—the way I've come to know the sea…as home.

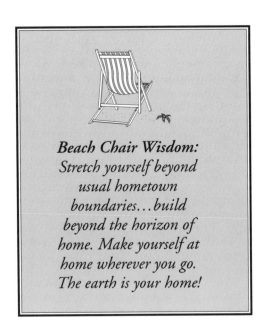

Beach Chair Wisdom:
Stretch yourself beyond
usual hometown
boundaries…build
beyond the horizon of
home. Make yourself at
home wherever you go.
The earth is your home!

An Occasional Nose-Dive Can Be Uplifting!

All right…I admit it! I do use the beach as my great escape. I doesn't take a mastermind to figure it out. I'm pretty easy to read, especially since I can be seen in shorts and a suntan all year 'round. And the sand in the floor mats of my car is probably a dead giveaway, too. If you were to look into the pocket of my khakis, you would find my favorite seashell. It's a little heart-shaped shell I found while walking the South Carolina sands. I always carry it with me. When I'm feeling the pressures of life, I pull that little shell out of my pocket. Ahhh…it takes me away to my very favorite place! It's the best little beach visit I can grab from five hundred miles away.

There is just something about the beach that makes me feel truly alive! There is nothing better for chasing away the blues than a walk on the beach in the warm sunshine. Even a grey day at the beach is wonderfully relaxing! I've thought about it a lot, and I believe the vastness of the ocean is just plain therapeutic. When you have the weight of the world on your shoulders, just stand on the shore and look out at the ocean. It makes any problem seem smaller, and you can't help but feel better. Look, too, at the countless grains of sand at the ocean's edge. The waves take that sand out with the tide, toss and turn it…and then put it back on the beach once again. There's no use fighting it; it's just the way it is. And, as soon as we figure out that life is not always smooth sailing, then we can skillfully learn to navigate through rough waters. Then we can, once again, dock safely at the shore.

Running away isn't always the best approach to life's problems. I should know…my little white sports car has over 100,000 beach miles on its odometer. I'm probably pretty close to an expert at driving away from troubles. But, in fact, I've found that running away rarely solves anything. But putting a little time and distance between you and your problems is probably a very healthy thing to do. Whenever I feel the pressures of home or work, I like to just get in my car and head south. I know that a beach trip is just what the doctor ordered.

As soon as I get in the car and start towards the beach, I feel better. And, as soon as I park my beach chair in the sand, I feel best! There is just something about it that makes everything bearable. The fresh ocean breezes help me to relax; and with the change of scenery, there are few thoughts of hometown problems. I just sit back and watch nature work her magic...on me.

While parked in my beach chair, I become a keen observer of nature. One of the seashore's most interesting creatures is the sandcrab. It is always amusing to watch a crab walk sideways, leaving broomlike tracks in the sand. Whenever someone approaches, the crab takes a quick nose-dive down into his hole. One day, the observation got me thinking that perhaps the sandcrab and I have something in common. And so, I watched more intently. And, as I watched, I thought more about my life. Were my beach trips a nose-dive from the responsibilities and worries of life? Was I dancing around problems and hiding out in my own personal hole? Was I running away or simply distancing myself? It was something to think about.

The sandcrab has the right idea, though. He comes out of his hole to live his coastal life. He steps out in faith onto those sands. When danger comes, he swiftly retreats to the safety of his hole. He is smart to take a detour from danger. When faced with the pressures and worries of life, it can be helpful to take a nose-dive of your own! Take some time and space for yourself...to think things through, to regroup, to gather strength and support—so that, in time, you can emerge on the sands...rested and ready to tackle your life again.

Of course, to be healthy, you can't live life in a hole. Even the sandcrab keeps his life in balance. And, balance is the key. Take time and space for yourself during the crunch times of life. An occasional nose-dive into the safety net of your own personal hole can be uplifting, indeed! But climb back out on the sands of life—rested and ready to live your life confidently and securely.

Beach Chair Wisdom:
Life was not meant to be lived in sandy isolation. Like the sandcrab, it's all right to retreat, from time to time, into the safety of your own personal hole. Space and time alone will help you to think things through and to gather the necessary strength and wisdom to meet the ongoing challenges of life. Remember...balance is the key!

Always Take Just One More Step!

Walking the beach is wonderfully invigorating. There is just nothing like it to start off your day. It's funny though…when I walk in my neighborhood at home, it's just not the same. I guess the pavement of hometown streets doesn't have the attraction of beachtown sands. The scenery along the shore is breathtaking! The sunlight sparkles on the water more brilliantly than diamonds, and the waves roll in to greet you as you walk. The pelicans fly by in formation, and your spirits soar with them in the coastal sky. And the fresh ocean breezes blowing through your hair seem to take all of your troubles on out to sea. All is right with the world! When I'm at home, I have to push myself to walk two and a half miles, five times a week. But, when I'm at the beach, I'm up early—ready to walk—every day. At the beach, the four miles to the pier and back seem like a walk around the block.

I do get tired sometimes. And when I do, I challenge myself. I've made it a personal challenge always to take just one more step. Every time I think I've walked as far as my legs will carry me, I go one more lap around the neighborhood or one more quarter-mile down the beach. It's been good to stretch myself beyond what I think are my limits. I've gotten into the wonderful habit of proving myself wrong. And that habit has been the right habit for me.

The lesson of always taking one more step has helped me to develop personal discipline that spills over into other arenas of my life. When I think I can't take the pressures of work one more day, when I think I can't hang on long enough to find the answer to a personal problem, when I feel as though I have no strength to go on…I take that important one more step. And I find I can get through another day, I can wait a little longer, I do have a bit more strength. I prove myself wrong by stretching myself beyond what I think I can do. Just when you think you can't go on, always take just one more step. It will prove you wrong, too…every time!

Life is hard. There is no denying it. And there are times we find ourselves struggling to cope with various deadlines, dilemmas, and difficulties of life. So it's important to train ourselves for those crunch times. We need to know that we are capable of handling anything that life sends our way. We need to trust our instincts and dig down deeply inside ourselves for the strength to go on…just one more step.

We all have our burdens to carry. At times, we trudge along the shoreline of life, feeling the weight of the world on our shoulders. We watch dark problem clouds roll offshore and relentless rain pound the sand. It seems as though this beach storm will last forever. But, when you least expect it, a break in the clouds appears. We get a small glimpse of the sun, and our outlook instantly changes. A weight is lifted from our shoulders, and we feel better. A smile begins growing across our faces and in our hearts. Everything seems possible now!

The truth is, beach storms don't last long. The grey clouds roll in, the rains pummel the shore, and the ocean breezes blow the storm on out to sea. It's great beach chair wisdom for all of us. When we really think about it, our personal storms don't last long, either. As Abraham Lincoln said, "Things get better. In fact, most things are better by morning." It's true. Whenever we think we can't handle a problem one minute longer, a break in the clouds appears. It may come to us through the smile of a friend, an encouraging word, a pat of approval, or our own personal discipline. Whatever form it takes, it helps us to go on…just one more step. And, that next step is an important step we all can take. We've got nothing to lose, and everything to prove!

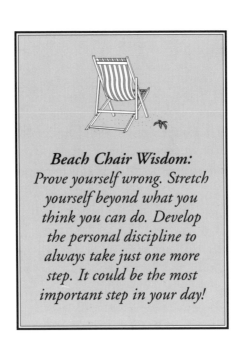

Beach Chair Wisdom:
Prove yourself wrong. Stretch
yourself beyond what you
think you can do. Develop
the personal discipline to
always take just one more
step. It could be the most
important step in your day!

Share Your Joy!

'll never forget the night that it happened. There I was, alone on the beach. The night sky was crystal clear. The stars seemed to jump out of the sky right before my eyes, and the crescent moon was strong enough to hang all my hopes on. It was early April of 1997...and comet Hale-Bopp was on the northwestern horizon. It was a magnificent show! The beach breezes were a perfect companion to this warm spring night. All was right with the world.

All of a sudden, a young boy ran out of the darkness and bounded right up to where I was sitting. "Can you believe how great this is?" he exclaimed. "This is a wonderful night," I responded with a smile. The little fellow was about eight or nine years old, running ahead of his parents. He was carrying a handful of shells and dumped them right out onto the sand beside me. He stopped to tie his shoe and to share a personal observation with this beachtown stranger. He was absolutely full of himself. "This is the first time I've ever seen the ocean!" he announced. "And, what do you think...?" I asked with joyful anticipation. "It's a miracle!" was his heartfelt answer. It was easy for me to agree. And, with his proclamation, I fell in love with the beach all over again!

Few times in life do we see such a clear-cut expression of true joy. And, when we do, it is definitely a contagious event. I never knew the little boy's name. He came in and out of my life as if he were in a revolving door. He disappeared as quickly as he came. But, he's with me now wherever I go, for we shared a very intimate moment—a moment of true joy. It's one moment in time that I'll always remember...and cherish.

Children know the true meaning of happiness. They live it every day. They are not inhibited by the hard knocks of life. Whenever they have a new experience, they bask in it with all of their senses. We adults have a lot to learn from children. That night on the beach taught me some valuable beach chair wisdom. Share your joy! Whenever you experience joy in your life, take the time to share it with someone else. It could be a family member or a friend, someone that you love or someone that you don't really know. But...share it. Share your joy!

I think back to the exceptional moments of happiness in my life…moments of true joy! Watching my sons be born, hearing "I love you" from that special person, getting unexpected good news from the doctor, hearing my parents tell me that they are proud of me, and feeling the hug of a kindergarten student around my knees. I have hundreds of memories of blessed moments like these. At each of those moments, I took the time to give thanks for the blessing. And, at each of those moments, I felt a tremendous need to share my happiness. I wanted to stand on a mountaintop and shout my joy. Sharing joy helps the world become a happier place. Joy shared is joy multiplied. It's a joyful lesson worth learning!

Joy is easy to spot. I've seen it many times on the beach. I've watched tenderly as a loving couple strolls the beach hand-in-hand. I've marveled when seeing a toddler whose toes touch the surf, perhaps for the first time. I've smiled with delight when an elderly gentleman passing by gratefully smiles back when I say hello. And, I've shared the pleasure of youngsters who giggle as their well-built sand castle withstands the threat of the incoming tide.

True joy! People say that there's not enough of it in the world, but I think there is enough of it to go around—if we would only share. The little boy on the beach taught me that. A walk on the beach later that same evening got me thinking…we can be the source of joy for others. It really doesn't take much effort. Just a little tuning in to others will set the stage. Take time out of your day to see things through the eyes of others. Look at life from a different perspective. The needs of others can be met…by the rest of us. If you see someone who needs a hug or a smile, give them one of yours. If you can ease the burden of a friend by listening, then offer both ears. An act of kindness never goes by unnoticed…or unappreciated. The joy it can bring can make someone's day. And it doesn't stop there. It makes the world a more joyful place…for everyone. So, as the old song encourages: joy to the world…joy to you and me!

Beach Chair Wisdom:
What the world needs now is
joy. Sharing helps the world become
a happier place. Joy shared is joy
multiplied. So…share your joy!

LESSON SEVEN

Build, Build, And Build...Again!

If I've learned anything from the seashore, it's the power of the human spirit. Standing on the shore, looking out over the ocean—it's easy to see the magnificent strength and power of the sea. The waves roll in and greet the shore with little interference. There's nothing we can do to stop their coming. High tides are hardly contained by the sand dunes and fences along the shore. There are days when the ocean tides are rough and relentless, and the ocean is a menace instead of a solace. When a storm comes, we are at the mercy of the sea. Its waves roar and rip at the coastline; the winds wreak havoc in partnership. We are left helplessly alone to watch and worry.

Hurricane Hugo pounded the eastern seaboard on September 22, 1989. South Carolina's Grand Strand was hardest hit. My family has a beach home right on that strand, in Garden City Beach. We sat at home in West Virginia and watched television accounts of the approaching storm. When the tropical storm was upgraded to a major hurricane, I listened to the worry in the voices of my parents. They were five hundred miles away and totally helpless to protect their seaside home. They could only wait and watch.

Wait and watch. Watch and wait…and worry. As predicted, Hurricane Hugo hit the area and hit hard! Hugo delivered a powerful punch all the way from Wilmington, North Carolina, to Charleston, South Carolina. Garden City Beach was not spared. Newspaper and television accounts painted a dismal picture of devastation in scores of coastal towns, including my favorite hideaway, Pawleys Island.

I was not there the day Hugo roared into town, but I visited the area several weeks later. What I saw changed me forever. Devastation loomed as far as the eye could see! Trees cradled fishing boats in their branches. Cars had blown onto rooftops. Concrete swimming pools at luxury hotels had been broken up and washed out to sea. On

Pawleys Island, I stood in stunned disbelief as I gazed at three houses all blown together in a heap. Everywhere I looked, residents were crying. They were sifting through the rubble of their lives. Their spirits were crushed, but not broken. They gained strength by working through this together to pick up the pieces of their lives.

I cried, too…for them. These beachtown strangers and I were bonded together by our humanity. I saw their faces, and I felt their pain. It left me lumpthroated and tender-hearted. Everywhere I went was the smell of disaster. The stench of dead fish and animals filled the air. Trees blocked most roadways, and parts of everything were…everywhere. The residents faced the overwhelming and seemingly impossible task of rebuilding. Just how to begin was the question.

The answer lay within. Deep within the recesses of the human heart and soul was something more powerful than the rage of the sea! The people of coastal South Carolina began digging. They dug deeply within themselves for the answer. And they found it—they found hope. And hope shared is hope multiplied. In September of 1989, the people of South Carolina found great power in their collective human spirit, in their collective hope.

America watched as Carolinians who had lost everything pooled their hope and pulled together. They started to rebuild in big ways and in small ways. They dug deeply into the earth and built new foundations for the future. It was amazing to see! The people of South Carolina used their spark of hope and growing determination to become the architects and builders of their destinies. It was a lesson in the power of the human spirit that has carried over onto the shoreline of my own life.

I, too, am an architect and builder. When I left the nest to build my own life after college, I drafted a blueprint for my life and began building. There have been several storms that ripped through my life and left personal devastation. Each time, I was faced with sifting through the wreckage for the pieces of my life. It was hard, but each time, my spirit triumphed over disaster! I set to work…building once again.

In life, the storms are many. Broken friendships and relationships are hurricane-strength storms we all may suffer at some point in our lives. Lost jobs, broken careers, and the deaths of loved ones leave us saddened and feeling stranded on shore. Broken promises and broken dreams leave us feeling, at times, like we cannot find the strength to rebuild to trust again. But if we dig deeply enough we can tap into the bottomless power of the human spirit. It can rise above the highest tides and the strongest winds. It gives us the resiliency to build, build, and build…again.

There's no limit to the number of times our castles in the sand can be washed out in the tide. And there's no limit to the number of times we can rebuild our lives with the hope that we carry in our hearts!

you are faced with a hurricane-strength storm in your life, know that you have the power within to withstand the rage of the sea. Deep within the recesses of your heart and soul, you carry a much stronger power…the power of the human spirit. Tap into it! Use that power to help you rebuild your personal sandcastles after the tides have washed away what you've worked so long to build. Rebuilding a life takes strength of character. And, that strength is found deep within each of us. The human spirit can always triumph over disaster!

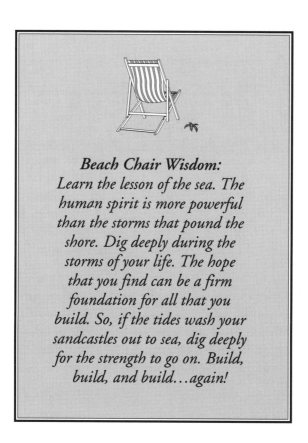

Beach Chair Wisdom:
Learn the lesson of the sea. The
human spirit is more powerful
than the storms that pound the
shore. Dig deeply during the
storms of your life. The hope
that you find can be a firm
foundation for all that you
build. So, if the tides wash your
sandcastles out to sea, dig deeply
for the strength to go on. Build,
build, and build…again!

Gentleness Is Sometimes The Truest Strength!

It was an incredible sight! Early one morning—just as dawn was breaking—I put on my running shoes and headed for the beach. I was prepared for a fast-paced four-mile walk to the pier and back. It was a gorgeous April morning, and the salt air beckoned in wonderful ways. I pulled my hair up in a ponytail, tied my shoelaces…and was off. Our beach house is about three blocks from the beach, so I was just getting into high gear when my feet hit the sand. All at once, I came to a complete standstill. Just for one fleeting moment in time, the scenery was almost unrecognizable. I shook my head in disbelief.

There was something very different about the ocean this spring morning. I plopped down in the sand just to take it all in. No ocean waves pounded the shore. In fact, the sea looked like the stillest lake I'd ever seen. The water was so calm—and a very deep blue. There was a beautiful silence surrounding the shore. The waves had ceased, the breezes had calmed…and what I saw changed me forever.

There, very close to the shore, in the calm waters—dozens of dolphins frolicked in play. They jumped through the air and dove back into the water, ever so gracefully. Floating on the still blue waters were all of the different shorebirds. Large and small, they had come together. Pelicans, usually so restless and on the prowl for food, relaxed and floated with ease. They were joined by seagulls and sandpipers. It was like a Monday morning meeting of nature…and it was the most beautiful sight! The sunlight sparkled on the water, illuminating this picture I'd keep forever in my mind. For this brief moment, there was true peace and harmony in nature. I marveled at the sight.

I sat in the cool morning sand as nature delivered her message. So this is how it's supposed to be. We are supposed to get along in the world in just this way…in real peace and harmony! Little by little, the morning beach visitors arrived. Children came, colorful buckets in hand, to explore the seaside sands. Adults unpacked their beach hairs and baskets. They opened their umbrellas to the sun. Lifeguards climbed to their duty seats overlooking the shore. I pulled myself up from my front-row seat—and started again on my walk towards the pier.

Gradually nature resumed her usual structure. The waves began rolling back to the shore, and the dolphins swam back out to sea. The pelicans headed to the south end of the island to the inlet creeks and marshes they call home. I walked on down the beach slowly and pensively…wondering if this were only a dream. An experience like this changes you forever. It's like heaven's door was thrown open for a moment, and I was allowed a small peek inside. I thought of the movie angel Michael's heavenly wisdom (from Lesson One) about listening to the earth. This time I was really paying attention! As I continued my walk, I thought about it a lot.

Back at home, I had been going through a trial. It was a trial of a professional nature—but it had hurt me deeply in very personal ways. I had been living under the personal microscope of a person who hated me. The hate was destroying her—and making my life more than difficult. Most days, I just went on with life, turning the other cheek. Some days were harder than others. The days and the weeks went on. They turned into years…in fact, twelve of them. I was tired of the struggle, and I was hoping that I could endure the trial without stooping to low levels of retaliation. I wanted to continue my journey on the higher road. But it was becoming increasingly more difficult. I wasn't sure how much longer I could go on.

As I walked towards the pier, I just kept thinking of that peaceful morning scene. I had been given a glimpse of nature's message about peace and harmony. I knew it wasn't by accident; I knew it was by grand design. Just when you think you can't go on in life, God always sends you just the message you need. That picture-perfect lesson was etched forever in my mind. Why couldn't my life be like that?

That April morning, the shorebirds and dolphins were all getting along. It was nature at its best! I knew that if I rolled up my sleeves and joined in the fight at home, that would be just as wrong as my opponent. I was determined to continue turning the other cheek. This perfect morning on the beach had shown me that I must not give up doing that.

I thought back to the trial I was under. Many friends had told me that this attack had gone on long enough. It was now time to fight back. One well-meaning friend reminded me that in some cultures my gentle response to my attacker would be perceived as weakness. The messages around me were all the same: "Perhaps it is time, Deb, to stand up for yourself."

It seemed like the last twelve years were crashing down on me all at once. Maybe it was time for a decision. And I did decide. After careful thought and deliberation, I decided on forgiveness. Although the last twelve years had worn me down, I discovered that something wonderful had happened. The twelve years of adversity had made me stronger! I now had the strength of character to make the right decision. My gentle and peaceful response had not been a weakness. It was a strength. It was strength of character!

I thank God for all of the wonderful messages He sent me along the way…smiles and support from friends, the desperately needed courage to do the right thing, and the wisdom to know that what had happened always told more about my opponent than i did about me. Just knowing that helped me get through a day. Then I found that I was able to get through another day…and another. Soon I had gotten through 4,380 days! My strong resolve to be gentle and peaceful had given me the power to endure the problems of my life without compromising my character. I am grateful for the wisdom and courage that helped me grow strong. And, now I'm a believer. At the beach and in life, gentleness can be great strength!

Beach Chair Wisdom:
When the trials and tribulations of life get you down, remember the beach scene on that perfect April morning. Turn the other cheek. And, when that doesn't work—try forgiveness. Peace and harmony are wonderful ways to live…for all of nature. In matters of character, gentleness is perhaps the truest strength!

Stand On The Horizon Of You!

No matter how you look at it, the view from the beach is incredible. I've driven the distinctive curve of the Pacific Coast Highway from Malibu to Santa Barbara and have been inspired by the majestic scenery. I've climbed the rocky cliffs of the New England coast and have been stilled with wonder. I've walked among the sea oats and sand dunes of the Carolina shore and have felt truly at home. From where I sit in a beach chair, any seashore is God's most brilliant masterpiece!

Over the years I've come, and I never tire of it. As a child I'd spend hours playing along the shore. With my plastic bucket and shovel, I'd dig in the sand tirelessly, hoping to find the treasures of the sea. Many times I'd come upon the "finds of a lifetime"—seashells, sharks' teeth, a broken sand dollar or two…even part of a cherished starfish. I remember a time when I was about seven years old when I found the most beautiful seashell. It was brown and white—and shiny and smooth. It was perfect in every way. I couldn't believe that, out of all the shells found on the beach that day, I would be so lucky as to find the best one of all. My grandmothers, Nanny and Nina, just smiled about the discovery. Little did I know how much of a gift they were really giving me that day!

While growing up, they made sure that I discovered more than the perfect seashell. Nanny and Nina ensured that I would come to discover the real treasure of the shore. Her beauty, her awe, her perfect balance…her wonder. That sense of wonder has sustained me for a lifetime. The beach is such a miracle of nature, how can we take any of it for granted?

As a child I loved the beach, but I also loved the sea. More than the usual summer tourist attractions, I loved the natural part of the shore. The sunlight sparkling on the water, the clouds over the horizon, the waves splashing on the rocks, the pelicans flying overhead…the shorebirds tickling the ocean surf on tiptoe. The smell of the salt air and the feel of the sea breezes blowing through my hair didn't hurt either. Ahhh! Just the thought of it takes me away!

As an adult, I quickly outgrew the commercial part of life around the shore. The older I got, the more I wanted to get away. Why would you need the hustle and bustle of crowds, traffic, pavilions, water slides, and amusement parks—when you could listen to the sounds of the sea? Those sounds are among nature's finest. The roar of the surf as it pounds the shore, the wind whistling through the palm trees, the squawk of the gulls overhead. Give me the solitude and sounds of nature, any day.

My November beach trip is always the best trip of the year. The tourists have gone home; the crowds and traffic have diminished. The amusement parks are boarded up for winter. All that is left is the sea. It's a heavenly transition. Let's head on back to the beach chair and think about it for a bit. The morning is foggy and cool, but a beach sunrise is always a good way to start the day. I look out over the horizon and await the morning miracle. The sun begins peeking out of the water right on schedule. Amazing! As the bottom of the morning sun clears the horizon, I offer my customary applause. I look around and wonder why the beach isn't filled with horizon-watchers witnessing this amazing, impressive event. Don't others realize the majesty of the moment?

Just looking out over the beach horizon makes me think about the horizons in life we see. Horizons can help us get the picture of what could be in life. Stand on your horizon and look. What do you see? Do you have a clear outlook—or are the distractions of life beginning to cloud your view?

I look out over the horizon and see the waves of life coming my way. I look in all directions. I see the home front and safety of the shore. I also see the adventure of the sea. They both call me. But one thing I know. We need to stand on our horizons and take a good look. A really good look. We need to think about the journey we want to take in life. We need to make a plan. We need to set goals. We need to chart direction. We need to learn to see past where and what we are—and see beyond…to where and what we can be! We need to seize that potential!

As I watch the sun over the coastal horizon, I think about the power of habits in our lives. If we choose to develop positive, constructive habits—we will build up our chances of a successful journey in life. We will be able to sail to wonderful places. If we choose to develop negative, destructive habits—we will tear down any chances we have of that successful journey. It would be like trying to sail the seas with a rickety old boat—full of holes. We surely wouldn't get far in life before our boat starts sinking. We would have no hope of sailing past our horizon.

What we need is a good compass for the journey. If we listen, learn, and live the character message in life, we will have the best compass of all—the character compass. It will surely guide us in the direction of reaching our true potential. With about ninety percent of what we do each day attributed to habit, we need to make sure that we are committed to the character habit. It's the only way to sail!

Beach Chair Wisdom:
Be a horizon-watcher!
Stand on your horizon
and look out over the
seas of life. What do you
see? Set your compass
and chart direction. If
you cultivate good
character traits and
habits in your life, you
will achieve more of
your true potential. Your
boat will sail successfuly
over the horizon—and
on to a wonderful you!

Sail On!

I'm comfortable at the seashore. Whenever I'm there, I feel right at home. It's fun to just kick off my shoes and settle in for a comfortable evening on the beach. I love to sit in my chair and bury my feet in the cool beach sand. The sand seems to call out to me, "Deb, take off your shoes. Take off your shoes!" And so…I do!

While I sit looking out over the sea, I think. Some of my best thoughts and ideas have been born at the beach. Those thoughts seem to roll in with the waves and blow in with the breeze. Listening to the earth is pure pleasure. Listening with my ears is only half of the story. When I'm at the beach, I listen with my heart! From that perspective, I've been able to hear some of nature's best messages.

Let's head down to the shore. Grab your ball cap because the winds are kicking up; the clouds seem to be rushing toward the horizon. The palmetto trees bend and sway in the excitement. Let's park our beach chairs here in the sand and watch for awhile. Without thinking, I kick off my shoes—and push my toes beneath the cool white sand. It feels just right! That old familiar feeling gets me thinking about a comfortable time from my past.

Years ago, I met a special person. From our first look we were drawn to each other. We kicked off our shoes, and talked—on into the night. We talked and laughed…we laughed and talked. We were just comfortable being together. Everything he said fascinated me. He would tell me about some wonderful idea he had, and I would add some much-welcomed insight. Before you knew it, we were off! Off on some brainstorming session that got us both excited about life.

Over the years, the friendship strengthened. We grew more and more comfortable with each other. It was a kick-off-your-shoes kind of togetherness. I considered that friendship a real gift in my life; I never, for one moment, took it for granted. Our talks were like basking in the coastal Carolina sunshine. They always made me feel warm and

...od all over. I looked forward to our visits like a little kid awaiting her first glimpse of the ocean. And, like the beach sunrises, each visit was new and unique…and beautiful.

The years went by. The more comfortable I got, the more I began to care about my friend. Just when I thought our friendship was as certain as the waves that roll to shore, beach winds began blowing in a different direction. An ocean storm was brewing out on the horizon. I never saw it coming.

Our last walk on the beach was different—and uncomfortable. My feet squirmed in the sand because I sensed my friend had something difficult to tell me. My fear of what he seemed to want to say made me feel as if the life were being choked right out of me. The beach rain began pouring down—and in my mind seemed to slap the sand fiercely. The waves seemed to be bringing me a painful rejection. There was nothing I could do to stop their coming. I couldn't stop my friend's words that hurt me so deeply. Our barefoot-on-the-beach friendship was over.

With one look I knew it was truly over—even my ocean of tears would not change his mind. He simply put on his shoes and walked down the beach…away from me. I will have to live the rest of my life with that memory carved painfully in my mind. As I sat there looking out into the coastal sky, I grieved. My loss felt as deep as the ocean. As much as I tried, I couldn't gather the strength to pick up my beach chair and go on. I sat on the sands of the past and cried.

I knew in my heart I couldn't spend the rest of my life just sitting there alone on that seemingly desolate beach. I knew I had to pack up my beach gear and board my boat…and resume my life. It was time to set my sails for new shores. I had to pull up anchor, untie my rope—and push away from that once-comfortable dock. I had to sail on! It was going to be hard…but I had to try.

Sometimes the winds of change blow into our lives. Often we're unprepared for their coming. We can try with all of our might to go against the wind, or we can simply turn and walk with it toward acceptance. We need to learn to accept the choices and decisions of others that so deeply affect our lives. Even when it's hard. Even when it hurts. Even when your heart is breaking. Even when you feel you'd rather die than try to go on.

Respect and acceptance are the survival skills that will help us navigate on the rough and challenging seas of life. Pulling up anchor required more strength than I thought I had in me. But I untied the rope, let it slip through my fingers…and sailed reluctantly towards the peace that I so desperately needed. It was one of the hardest things I've ever had to do. And it hurt in ways that I'll always remember. As long as there are stars in the heavens, as long as waves roll on to the shore, I'll never get over the loss of him in my life.

But the Keeper of the Stars has His plan. I have to believe on faith that His plan includes me. As long as I live, I'll keep searching for that one, kick-off-your-shoes kind of friendship that I can call home. Until then, I'll just sail on!

Beach Chair Wisdom:
There are times in life when we
are fortunate enough to have that
kick-off-your-shoes kind of belonging and
togetherness with someone we really care
about. Cherish each of those blessed
moments. If the winds of change blow
into your life, adjust your sails towards
acceptance and peace…and sail on!

Life Ebbs And Flows!

f you haven't seen it, you've just got to go—it's the sight of a lifetime. But timing is
ally important to witness it properly. You've got to make plans. Pack up your beach
ar, and don't forget your camera. This is something that you'll always want to
member. We're off to the beach to await the moonrise.

ow, don't get me wrong. The sunrise on the eastern shore is magnificent. I try never
miss one when I'm at the beach. But when the full moon is scheduled to rise from
e Atlantic Ocean, I want a front-row seat. Last night I saw it—and it was spectacular!
saw the full harvest moon rise out of the beautiful blue sea. In a word…it was breath-
king! The moon was big and round and orange…and perfect. I sat in the cool evening
nd and waited. At exactly 8:41 p.m.—just as scheduled—it came up. Without fanfare
grand announcement of any kind, it simply did its thing. It rose.

love the moon. I've had a lifetime love affair with that big white circle in the night
y. From the time I could talk, I have been asking to see the moon at night before
ing to sleep. From the crib I would call out to see the "boon," and my parents
ould take me to the window for a child-size glimpse of the moon that stilled me with
onder. These long years later, looking for the moon is still the last thing I do each
ght before going to bed.

he rising moon is grand. And if your timing is right, an ocean moonrise can be the
ing on your coastal cake. Just sit and watch as it rises right out of the water and takes
place in the evening sky. The blues and greys of evening are streaked with pinks
d purples. It's a sight for a beach bum's eyes! So tonight I went back for a repeat
rformance. Clouds were beginning to gather on the horizon. Sometimes the clouds
ll block your view of this spectacular event—and other times the clouds will frame
ur view of the moonrise in wonderful ways.

I sit and watch the moon, I am reminded of the tides. At our beach house, we have a
e clock. It helps us plan our days at the beach by indicating when the high tides will
me to force us back home. Garden City Beach has been different in recent years. After
rricane Hugo pounded the area in 1989, beach access has been limited. The storm

took away much of the sand, and left a more narrow beach for coastal residents. When high tides come, the waves roll right up to the sand fences onshore, which is more than disturbing to the owners of beachfront property. More than ever before, high tides crowd this shore. But when low tide comes, all is right with the beach! The waves retreat and leave lots of sandy beach for everyone to enjoy.

There are some who love low tides most. In the Harbor Talk newsletter from Georgetown, South Carolina, I quote an unnamed author: "High tide gets the glory, while nothing good is ever said about the low tide." The author goes on to quote Shakespeare, Charles Dickens, and John F. Kennedy to support the premise. The whole point of the article is to point out the goodness of low tide: "And don't forget the sandpipers flitting up and down the beach at low tide, the fiddler crabs happily scampering in and out of their holes, the egrets and herons preparing to spear dinner, the 'doubler' crabs mating on the pilings. It all happens at low. Think I'm a low tide fan? You guessed it; I'll take a low anytime. But I've been running against the tide most of my life anyway." What coastal wisdom! Here is a person who has learned to make the best of every situation life offers.

I've thought of how life is like the tides. Whether you prefer high tide or low tide, neither one lasts. Each is only part of the cycle, and you must go through the other to get your favorite back. Soon the waves of life start rolling in and fill up our lives with new adventures and challenges.

I love the sea, both its low tides and high tides. I savor them both as a part of life. During the low tides in my life, when I'm feeling loss, I have taken solace in being near the sea. During the high tides, my life has been filled with adventure, successes, and triumphs. I love those times, but I know they're only part of the cycle. The cycle must complete itself, the high tide must retreat to the sea. Just as the best part of the moon comes and goes, so do the tides. I await their coming.

Beach Chair Wisdom:
Life is like the ebb and flow of
the tides. So give in to nature
and learn to enjoy the cycle.
Goodness can be found at every
tide. If you look for the best in
nature, you will find it!

Charting Your Course Means Charting Your Destiny!

n Murrells Inlet, South Carolina, I love to go to the marina just to watch the boats.
The old wooden docks seem to call out to me to sit for awhile to take in the sights. But
don't be fooled. I take in the smells of the marina as well. At the end of day, the shrimp
boats come home with their catch of the day. The lobster traps and fishing nets being
hauled to shore make the old docks come alive with activity. The gulls swarming and
squawking overhead complete the perfect coastal picture. When I'm at the marina, all is
right with the world!

The Gulf Stream Café is my favorite seafood restaurant there. It sits at the edge of the
marina overlooking the coastal inlet marshes. With the beach to its front, and the creek
to its back, it has scenery from the best of both worlds. The food is almost as good as
the sunset over the ocean creeks! My sister Ellen and I spent a wonderful evening at The
Gulf Stream last summer. We went early to get a table by the window. Yellowfin tuna
grilled medium-rare, garlic mashed potatoes, fresh asparagus, hot homemade crusty
bread, key lime pie, and an inlet sunset—what more in life could anyone possibly want?
The salt-water smell from the marina blowing through the open cafe windows was the
proverbial icing on the coastal cake.

Ellen and I sat for what seemed like forever. We sat taking in all of the sights, smells,
and tastes of the ocean evening. It was one of the most wonderful dinners I've ever had
at the beach. The atmosphere and the food were perfect, and we talked and laughed—
about everything. We really had fun. After dinner we walked outside and took in the
night salt air. Ahh…what a fabulous smell!

We stood looking out over the inlet creeks, watching the evening sunset fade into the
horizon. The stars began to dot the late summer sky. It made me think of how
important those stars really are. I thought of how the early sailors used those same
stars to chart direction for their travels. Stars really can show us the way! A treasured
quote from Ralph Waldo Emerson came to mind: "Hitch your wagon to a star." Over
the years, I seem to have written my own beach-style version of his thought: Hitch
your boat to a star. Anyway you look at it, it's great wisdom!

I went to bed that evening listening to the sounds of the seashore. From my bed, I coul[d] hear the roar of the ocean as if it were my lullaby for the night. It was as if I were lying on a bed of sand, and the gentle ocean breezes were rocking me to sleep. Whenever I'm at the beach, I always sleep like a baby…a beach baby!

As I slept, I dreamed of the sea. I dreamed of my course in life and my destiny. I awoke with life—its meaning and my purpose—foremost on my mind. I thought of how my beach trips are always spent in thoughts as deep as the ocean. At home I could swim around in a pool all day, and come up dry of ideas. But there is just something about the seashore that gets my creative juices flowing. Like a little kid filled with anticipatio[n] over a drive to the shore, I always know that once I'm here, I'll be filled with exciteme[nt] and wonder over my new plans for life.

I pulled on my shorts and a tee shirt, and headed on down to the beach. As the sun ros[e] up over the Atlantic Ocean, I saw a fishing boat head out to sea. I thought about the discipline of those fishermen who are up early each day, off on the seas in search of the[ir] livelihood. I do not take their daily work and efforts for granted. Especially grateful fo[r] the boats that bring yellowfin tuna and flounder back to shore, I smiled in sincere appreciation. I thought about all of the different journeys that we take in life. Educational journeys, career journeys, personal and professional journeys…and journeys of the heart. I believe that all of these journeys require a plan. We must make [a] map of our desired destinations; we must chart our way. I remembered a quote on a desk calendar by Stephen Covey: "If you are an effective manager of self, your disciplin[e] comes from within: it is a function of your independent will. You are a disciple, a follower, of your own deep values and their source." It was food for thought. In fact, it was seafood for thought!

Our journeys in life require good planning. First we have to decide where in life we want to go. We have the choice of going toward good destinations in life—or toward destinations of a less honorable nature. The choice is ours. We are the navigators of our own ships. Let's take Covey's idea a little further and blend it with the Emerson quote. When we do, we come up with even more beach chair wisdom: When you hitch your boat to the guiding star of good character, you become a natural follower of your own deep values. So when sailing on the seas of life, chart your journey by the stars. Charting your course means charting your destiny. Go towards goodness!

Beach Chair Wisdom:
Hitch your boat to a guiding star! It's the best compass for charting your direction in life. With the star of good character as the compass and guide for all you do, you will chart your course towards the goodness in life. Charting your course means charting your destiny!

Discover New Oceans!

One evening on Pawleys Island, I grabbed up my beach chair and notebook and headed for the water's edge. It was a perfect evening. The surf was calm and serene and blue. The water gently hugged the rocks along the shoreline, as pelicans flew low over the ocean's spray. A most welcome breeze accompanied the approaching sunset, and all was right with the world.

Thinking about it made me realize how comfortable I am here on the sand. I always feel at home here. Perhaps it's the warm autumn sky with its pinks and greys and blues. Maybe it's the warm salt air that takes all of my tensions away. Maybe it's just the beauty and wisdom of nature at its best. All I know is that, when I'm here, I'm deeply content.

Being uncomfortable is never easy. We've all experienced the feeling, and I'm sure that we all work quite hard to avoid uncomfortable situations. While reading over a collection of quotes, I saw this one by André Gide: "You cannot discover new oceans unless you have courage to lose sight of the shore." It got me thinking about growing too comfortable in life.

If I chose to sit on these sands and enjoy my comfortable existence of life-by-the-sea, I would do little growing. How could I possibly stretch myself beyond the comfortable boundaries of my beachtown existence if I stayed right in this chair? Sure, it would seem like a safe and protected life. I could sit right here and have this same, familiar perspective of the ocean for the rest of my days. Or I could get up, pack up my chair, and get moving in new directions. I could become like the sailors and explorers we've read about in our school history books. I could leave the shore and begin charting a new direction.

One thing about being comfortable is that it makes us feel safe. But it also keeps us in place. We find comfort when we're set in our ways, our habits, our routines. There's a certain amount of pleasure in this level of comfort. But can we discover anything new about ourselves and the world around us if we never stretch ourselves at all?

Think of the wonderful story of Christopher Columbus. Growing up in the seaport town of Genoa, Italy, young Chris spent his free time sitting on the docks and watching ships come in and out of port. He dreamed of one day sailing on one of those big ships—and charting a new direction for his life. More than anything, he wanted to be a sailor. And nothing would stand in the way of his dreams. As a young man, Columbus spent years trying to get a ship, crew, and supplies for his maiden voyage. He was turned down by the unsupportive king and queen—and waited literally years for his answer. Columbus' desire to go in search of new oceans was no match for the royal naysayers. Finally, Columbus' wish was granted, and he set sail on the adventure of a lifetime!

Does that mean Columbus' travels were smooth sailing from then on? No. It just means that he showed the good character traits of patience, determination, persistence, commitment, and hard work in achieving his dream. Young Columbus showed courage in losing the sight and safety of the shore in his quest to discover new oceans. And we all know that he discovered much more than that!

With all of these thoughts going through my mind, my beach chair on Pawleys Island was starting to feel a little uncomfortable. Yes, I do tend to hide away here from time to time. It is my small, but important, escape from my busy life. After a short respite on my beloved island, I feel more ready to leave sight of the shore and set sail on my own new adventures. Stretching myself beyond my comfort level is a wonderful way to grow. And, by applying the positive traits of trustworthiness, respect, responsibility, and caring to the adventure—it becomes a wonderful way to grow in character.

As the sun set over the inlet waters, I packed up my chair and notebook and put them in the trunk of my car. I took a short walk to the south end of the island. The beach was empty now. The few seaside residents had already started for home. Begging moments before the day's end, I stood looking out over the sea. The ocean looked so big and so overwhelming—just like life, at times. I thought about the explorers and sailors throughout history who have sailed these very seas. I admire and respect their courage and their character.

It's a lesson for all of us: Nothing ventured, nothing gained. Get too comfortable, and life just passes us by. With bold Columbus on my mind, I turned and headed for my car. Just then, I spotted a tiny light—way out on the horizon of the sea. Another sailor must be sailing towards his dream. That night before going to bed, my mind was filled with thoughts of adventure. I would take Columbus' dream with me to my sleep. After all, we are kindred spirits. His life was not much different from mine. I love the water, I love the ships. And I, too, am a dreamer. I drifted off to sleep that night excited about my next adventure!

Beach Chair Wisdom:
Being comfortable is not always a wonderful thing. Stretch yourself beyond your usual beachtown and hometown boundaries. Like Columbus, we have to be willing to leave the sight and safety of the shore. Then we can chart new adventures in courage…and character!

Rough Seas Make
Good Sailors!

t was a beautiful autumn Sunday morning. Sunlight sparkled through the trees,
accenting the magnificent colors of red and gold. The sky was a deep September blue,
and the fallen leaves were blowing in the gentle breeze. The crickets sang their hymns
of the season, as families walked the sidewalks of town towards church. I had spent
the early morning hours writing a lesson for this book. I turned off my computer and
decided to take a drive into town. I was on my way to the post office to mail a letter to
a friend, when I turned the corner by the fire station in town—and saw the idea for
my next lesson staring me in the face. It was a church marquee on a hometown street
carrying a beachtown message: *Calm seas never made great sailors.* I knew it was
beach chair wisdom. I couldn't wait to get home to write about it!

I immediately thought about something similar that my friend Phil had once told me.
I was having a particularly tough time at work. It seemed that the waves were hitting
me from all directions. I was struggling just to keep my head above water. Phil had said
simply and reassuringly, "Deb, rough weather makes for good timber." Phil grew up
in North Carolina, and he loves the mountains like I love the seashore. His wisdom,
although a little different from mine, carries the same message from nature: Challenges
help us grow strong. I got excited just thinking about it. Sure, smooth sailing is always
a wonderful part of life. But, just how much could we possibly grow in wisdom and
strength of character if everything always went smoothly? It was a wonderful revelation
for me this crisp and beautiful morning.

Life is like the sea. A calm sea is fun to enjoy. Smooth sailing is relaxingly wonderful—
and a very much needed part of life. We need to have days and weeks when our sailing
is on calm and peaceful waters. But a calm sea does little to challenge us and help us
grow. There are times when we seem to be pulled in by the swift ocean tides and pulled
under by the powerful currents. The rough seas toss and turn us with unrelenting effort.
That's when our navigational skills are put to the test—and that's when we learn and
grow the most.

I thought back to a television show that I had seen. A little girl's grandfather had passed away, and she was saying a few words about him at the memorial service. During her eulogy to her grandfather, this eleven-year-old girl told her family and friends about the life lessons her grandfather had taught her. Marah went on to say that what she remembered most was the lesson about jumping the waves. Her grandfather had taken her by the hand, and together they had walked down to the seashore. When the waves rolled in, they jumped and jumped. Many times Marah and her grandfather had cleared the waves. But, yes…there were times when the waves knocked them down. Marah's grandfather was very wise to teach her to get up and to try again. From spending that day with her grandfather, Marah was convinced that jumping the waves of life would help you become successful at everything you tried to do. What wonderful beach chair wisdom for all of us: Learn to jump the waves!

Life sends many waves our way. Some are like the day-to-day challenges that we all experience. They come and go just as quickly as the waves on the shore. Learning to jump the waves can help us as we face those daily challenges. But sometimes the challenges we face are of a more serious and long-lasting nature. That's when we must learn to navigate over rough and unyielding seas. We need to learn to ride out the tougher times in life. That's when our resiliency skills are most important. Don't give up! Be a determined and diligent sailor. The storm will subside. Smoother sailing will come in the days and weeks ahead.

Beach Chair Wisdom:
Remember that calm seas
never made great sailors.
Expect some rough waters on
the journey of life. These
challenges will help you grow
and develop your character.
And when the next storm comes,
you'll be stronger and more
skilled…more able to handle
whatever comes your way!

Leave your troubles here at the water's edge, and let's walk the beach for a bit. Let's think about the power of the sea. The inhabitants of the shore have to take whatever comes their way. It's a natural part of living by the sea. When all is sunny and calm, it's a wonderful life. When a tropical storm approaches, it's time to take on the challenge of weathering the rough and powerful sea. At times like these, all you can do is board up your house and ride out the storm.

Whether we are sailing on the water or living ashore near it, we have to weather the storms of life. They are unavoidable. By rising to the challenge, we will become stronger and more resilient—able to handle whatever life sends our way. Stay strong! As you grow in courage, you grow in character!

No Man Is An Island!

Pawleys Island, South Carolina, is a beautiful place. If I had to pick my very favorite spot in the whole world, it would be Pawleys. Now, don't get me wrong. I haven't been all around the world. Not even close. But there is something about Pawleys Island that tells me I need look no further. Deep in my heart, there was a connection with us from the very beginning. It was just love at first sight!

The first time I drove to Pawleys, I crossed the bridge to the island and smiled. I was pleasantly surprised to see that it was simply built and "arrogantly shabby." There is no commercial development on the island, just private homes and beach rentals. It's a narrow barrier island—perhaps five or six miles long, framed by the beach on the east, and by saltwater creeks and marshes on the west. Residents walk and ride bicycles on the island road, escaping the hustle and bustle of real life just a few miles away on the mainland. The sun sets over the island creeks in the west and casts an orange glow that reflects over the ocean waters. All is right with the world!

Walking on the south end of the island is like walking on your own private beach. It's a picturesque walk along the sea oats and sand dunes to the end of the island. The waves roll in to greet you as if you were the only visitor of the day. There have been many days when I found myself alone on the beach for hours at a time. Just me and the shorebirds and pelicans. Not a bad way to spend the day.

Autumn is my favorite time there. The summer crowds have gone, as vacationers have traded their beach dreams for the realities of responsibility and work. Every year I savor each of my nine November days there. Talk about pure pleasure! I take my beach chair, journal, blue pen, and Cherry Coke® to the beach—and I'm ready for the great adventure of spending the day alone. As sea breezes blow through my hair, all of my stresses and troubles drift out to sea. I bask in the luxury of being alone in the relaxing sunshine. Ahh…this must be heaven!

Here I get to think. It's a simple as that. Time to think, time to feel…time to enjoy the solitude of it all! Some of my best moments are times I spend with just me. I guess that must sound a little funny. But, if I'm not good company for me, how could I possibly be good company for anyone else? That very thought got me thinking…about our need for solitude and our inherent need to be near and with other people. We've heard the wisdom before: No man is an island. It's true. Although we do need our own time and space, we need the companionship and camaraderie of others to make it in this world. We need to be connected.

So as I sat one day in the beach chair looking out over the ocean, I thought of that connectedness. It's a critical part of human existence. It suddenly dawned on me that the oceans of the world are all connected. They each have their own space and boundaries, yet they connect with each body of land and with each other…and connect our homelands, one to the other.

Just as solitude is a necessary part of life, so is connectedness. It's great beach chair wisdom. No man is an island. We really need each other in life. Perhaps the difference between going it alone and being connected to others is the same as the difference between existing and really living. It might just be as simple as that. In nature, the bodies of water are all connected. The rivers flow through the land to meet the ocean, and the oceans of the world all connect. Just south of Cape Horn, at the bottom of South America, the Atlantic and Pacific oceans meet. Their conflicting winds and currents tumble together to make this the roughest, most feared stretch of water in the world. There the waves toss and turn wildly in confrontation!

Life is like that. People who live and work together meet on a common ground. And, since we all come to our encounters with different currents of intention, at times it can be a real wave-making experience. But our attitudes will determine how we will handle the meeting of the minds. Are we respectful of the opinions of others? Are we comfortable enough with ourselves to not feel threatened? Can we step back from the safety and comfort of our own solitude to enjoy our connectedness with other people?

Perhaps we can learn a lesson from the wisdom of the sea. For all of us, there's a coming together and a going apart—a time of connectedness and a time of solitude. For both, we should all be grateful. For each opportunity gives us a chance to grow, a chance to reach our true potential, and a chance to carve out our own character…and destiny.

I believe that life was not meant to be lived alone. We need each other. And though we sometimes come together with competing winds and currents, we must blend eventually. It's up to each of us to assume responsibility for others. It's up to each of us to exercise the good character traits of citizenship, civility, and caring for our family and friends of the earth. Like the oceans of the world, we are all connected…connected by our humanity. It's a connection worth celebrating!

Beach Chair Wisdom:
There is a time for solitude and
a time for coming together.
Celebrate one of the best parts
of the human experience…
our connectedness. Remember,
no man is an island!

Our Decisions Define Us!

Decisions, decisions! Do you get ever caught up in the whirlwind? Decisions come at us from all directions. They range from the simple to the complex, from the trivial to the vital. We probably make more decisions in the course of a day than we even realize.

Deciding on a beach trip is never difficult for me. Whenever I can get away, I do! Deciding on what to pack is never given a thought. A few pairs of khaki shorts, my tennis shoes and ball cap, my beach journals, and some music for the road...and I'm off. It's as simple as that. No worries, no responsibilities, no decisions. It's beach time! Perhaps, getting away from it all means not only getting away from the responsibilities, worries and pressures of life...but also the decisions!

Pull up a beach chair beside me, and let's think about it a bit. As I look out over the ocean, I see the flat September clouds drifting by in the warm salt air. The blues today are many. Even the designers at Crayola would be impressed at the beauty of these colors in the sky. The evening sun is beginning to dip towards the west, as the pinks and purples begin seeping into the evening sky.

Twilight...my favorite time of day. Many evenings I come to sit and watch the sky grow dark. It's an amazing event! Off in the distance, pelicans fly towards the south end of the island...back to the inlet creeks and marshes they call home. The seagulls and sandpipers crouch at the water's edge. The tides soften as the harvest moon pulls them back away from shore. The sands swirl and the palmetto trees sway in autumn breezes. The sand crab takes twilight's last dive into his hole. A lone sailboat on the horizon makes the turn for land. A few people are walking the beach as a way to end their day. Soon, they'll go to the safety and comfort of home.

It's easy to breathe here. I relax and take in the sights. I think about the definition of the sea. The ocean is defined by the shoreline, and the land is defined by the sea. From time to time, the rage of the sea overtakes the land. The power of an angry sea redefines the shoreline. But after the storm, the sea retreats back within its boundaries. All of nature is defined within the balance. I marvel at the plan. Then, I think about us. What defines us, what makes us who we are? Just what gives definition to the human character? All of a sudden, in the encroaching darkness of evening, my own lightbulb comes on. Decisions define us. It is our decisions that carve out our character.

A friend, Dr. William Mitchell, once told me that we never know which decisions in li are the important ones, but we can count on the fact that each little decision we make will add up in big ways to determine who we become. He's right. Our character is not determined in one year, one day, one act, or one decision. It's determined by the way w live each day! Every thought, decision, and action add up to determine the kind of person we become. So, every decision for us is a defining moment!

I guess I had it pegged all wrong. I'd been thinking that only the big decisions in life were the important ones. I suppose I had never given much credence to the power of the little decisions that we make throughout the course of a day. But those little decisions probably pave the way for the bigger decisions we meet further on down the road of life. If we make good choices early on, I just bet we won't have to face decisions of much larger proportions later on.

I have faced some big decisions in my life. Decisions that taunted and tormented me. Decisions that wouldn't let me rest. But, after the decision was finally made, I was able to think back. All along I knew just what to do, the choice I should make. I knew in m heart that I should choose the right thing to do. I knew I should go with my conscienc

Recently I struggled and struggled with a major life decision. I knew what was right, b I let the details distract me and get me down. There were extenuating circumstances. There were exceptions to the rule. Feelings were involved. I wrestled with what seemed right for me…and what was RIGHT. The struggle became fierce. It consumed me. Going on deep within my soul was the fight of a lifetime. The fight raged on, between doing what I wanted and needed to do…and what I should do. I'll have to be honest and say, it was not a pretty sight. Sometimes, my humanness does not become me.

To win the battle and strengthen myself, I headed for the beach. I knew all along that I carried within me the strength of character needed to make the right decision. But I needed some time and space and a fresh perspective from the beach chair. I took shelter in life-by-the-sea and tapped into nature's wisdom. Looking out at the vastness of the sea helped me put my problem into perspective. I was able to gather the courage to choose rightness. I needed to go to the next step beyond the knowing… to the doing. Before, in my life, it had always seemed a whole lot easier. This time was different.

I wish I could say that, after all that thinking and struggle, I readily chose the right path. I didn't. My heartstrings pulled me in a different direction. It took some time…a very long time. After many months of introspection and struggle, I chose to do the rig thing. It was perhaps the hardest thing I've ever had to do. Oh, don't get me wrong! I

anted to do the right thing—I really did. But this time it meant great personal
crifice. In the end, that's what I chose. The intrinsically good feeling that came
ommaking the right decision eased my loss. It took some time…lots of time. But it
d happen.

hat painful decision gave me power, the power to make more good decisions in my
e. The strength and structure of my character has developed in direct proportion to
at decision. It is one lesson that will stay with me for life. Now, when I walk the
ach, at least I'm in the good company of a better and stronger person—me!

Beach Chair Wisdom:
Tune into the definition and
balance of nature. Know that
big or small, each decision
you make in your life is a
defining moment. Don't give
up during the important
decision-making times of your
life. Dig down inside yourself
for the strength of character
needed to make the right
decision. Deep within, you have
the power to go from
the knowing to the doing.
Remember, you'll have to live
with each decision you make!

If Your Ship Doesn't Come In...
Start Swimming!

I love old docks—especially old, creaky wooden docks. In fact, the older they are, the better. I have a friend who lives on breathtakingly beautiful Lake Norman, near Charlotte, North Carolina. Some of my favorite memories are there on the old wooden docks. There's nothing like a lake sunset from one of those docks. The smell of the wood, the smell of the water, and the feel of evening's best breezes in your hair —are simply amazing. I love to sit back and watch Mother Nature's best colors light up the sky. Yellows…to oranges…to reds…to pinks…to purples. It's a wonderfu treat to sit and watch these magnificent Crayola sunsets with a friend. It's the perfect way to end the day. As each star comes out in the evening sky, another problem in life disappears into the night. Ahh…just thinking about it takes me away!

One sunny February day I was there. I took my journal and headed for the dock. It w easy for me to write there. The sunlight sparkled on the water, as the sailboats sailed ir and out of the marina. The clips on the masts of sailboats clanged in harmony with th lake breezes, and all was right with the world! I could have stayed forever.

Later, I found myself giving in to the call of an afternoon nap. Right there on the dock! It was so warm and so peaceful, I just couldn't resist. I put my journal aside and stretched out in the warm winter sunshine. The sun felt so good on my face as I closec my eyes and drifted off to sleep. When I woke up, I found that I was in the good company of nature. A few ducks and a rather large turtle had shared my spot in the afternoon sun.

In recent years, there has been great commercial development in the Lake Norman are Everyone wants to move there. The wooden docks at the marina have been updated ar replaced with more modern and sturdy concrete docks. I suppose that some would cal this progress. I call it an unfortunate mistake. The docks have lost their character and ppeal. They no longer seem warm and inviting. Sure, the new docks do the job of elping sailors board their boats for a day on the lake. But they no longer call out to hose of us who like to sit for awhile to watch and to dream. Luckily for me, there is still ne wooden dock. Like a favorite old sweater or pair of sneakers, it fits me just right. hat wooden dock at Lake Norman has many special memories of mine carved right nto its planks. These many years later, I still feel welcome whenever I stop by for a visit.

imilarly, I love old docks in coastal towns. Whether extending into a lake or the ea, the appeal is the same for me. When I sit on one, I always feel right at home. ll day long, boats sail in and out. I have watched many times, wishing for a sailboat f my own. I've thought about the things in life we all wish for—if not a boat, other mportant things we want to have or achieve. Our hopes, our dreams, and our oals are like those boat-wishes. We sit on the docks of life and look out over the vater…watching and wishing. Boats sail by: opportunities, hopes, answers, friends, areers, solutions, achievements. Often we watch and wait for those boats to come to ur dock. It doesn't take much effort to figure out that the things we want most in life lon't just magically appear on our doorsteps, nor do these boats end up docking n our own personal marinas.

onrad Hilton once wisely penned, "If your ship doesn't come in, swim out to it." ather than watching and waiting for your ship to come to you, swim out to your ship! t takes determination and strength of character to make your dreams come true. It also akes responsibility, hard work, perseverance, courage, sacrifice, and commitment. If it vere easy to achieve our heart's desires, they would mean little. Life would become neaningless, and we'd become dissatisfied in no time at all. Setting goals and working liligently towards them gives real fire and passion to our dreams! Swimming out to ur boats is much more rewarding than having them show up at our docks narked "SPECIAL DELIVERY."

apoleon Hill and Clement Stone's writings have taught us that we can believe and chieve. The work of Dr. Norman Vincent Peale, Dr. William Mitchell, and Michael Mitchell have taught us the value of a positive attitude in reaching for our dreams. I elieve that a positive attitude, belief in self, and goal setting are the foundations for all uccesses in life. But it's strength of character that enables us to swim out to our own oats and to bring them to our dock.

o here we sit on the wooden dock, looking out over the water. Say that on the horizon ou see the boat of your dreams! Do you simply sit there, with your feet dangling in the vater, and hope that it sails your way? Or do you take action? Do you get up from the lock and gingerly wade out into the water? Or do you dive right in?

o be honest, I've spent much of my life diving right into the water. And as I swam out o reach that boat, I've gone under many times, sometimes struggling just to tread water. But so many times I've reached my desired boat—drenched, out of breath, and exhausted. But what sweet satisfaction! There's such exhilaration and power in the effort! Those boats I swam out to meant everything to me because of the hard work and sacrifice involved.

So when you see the boat of your dreams on the horizon, don't just watch and wait. Go after it! Swim out to it! The reward is far greater for the effort.

Beach Chair Wisdom:
Think about the things in life
that you want. It takes wisdom and
strength of character to make your
dreams come true. It also
takes responsibility, hard work,
perseverance, courage, sacrifice,
and commitment. Don't just sit
on the dock and see what might
happen. When your boat appears
on the horizon, dive right in
and start swimming!

Catch Good Character Traits In Your Net!

All right, I admit it! I've gotten into the habit of going to the beach. Spring, summer, fall, and winter...I just have to go! My jaunts to the beach have become an irresistible, but treasured habit. Last November was the first year of the last twelve that I didn't get in my car and head south. Oh, I wanted to. But life got in the way of my plans. Missing this November beach trip was hard for me. With three days left in the month, there is a small part of me that wants to jump in my car...and go. I guess until I had to miss it, I didn't really know how ingrained in me that November trip was.

Through my association with Mike Mitchell, my beach friend and mentor, I have learned the importance and power of habits in our lives. Mike and his dad, Dr. William Mitchell, have taught me that our attitudes determine our actions, and our actions determine our habits. Research tells the story: Habits account for ninety to ninety-five percent of what we do each day. It's a powerful reminder to be careful about the habits that we choose to develop. Anyone who has tried to break a bad habit knows the monumental struggle it can be.

I believe our character is built on a foundation of habits. We can work toward the honesty habit—or give in to the habit of hedging the truth. We can develop the habit of caring and service to others—or take the easy way out by cultivating a self-serving habit. We can develop the habit of being responsible—or of being irresponsible. It really is up to us. Our habits come from our decisions, and our decisions define us. Our habits help define us as people of character—or as people without.

Habits are the driving force behind most of our day-to-day thoughts and actions. We go through many of the motions of daily life and work without really thinking. Because of these habits, we become very comfortable with our daily behaviors. We're used to acting a certain way. Until something happens to cause us to step back and think about our habits, we just keep on living our lives under their direction.

One day while reading, I came across a wonderful quote from Sterling W. Sill: "A determined person allows no exceptions to success. Exceptions tear down a success habit faster than victories can build it up." Wow! What an inspirational thought! I revised it a little to apply it to the character message: A person of good character allow no exceptions to doing the right thing. Exceptions tear down a character habit faster than doing right can build it up. It's wonderful wisdom to think about!

Character development is a lifetime journey. We are either people growing in characte and goodness—or we aren't. But that doesn't mean that any of us is perfect. We are all human, and we all make mistakes. We are people who try, who struggle, who fail, and who get up and try again. I have heard it said that you can tell a person's true characte by what he does after he makes a mistake. It is hard work to develop the character hab There are no magic wands to help get us there.

That's where the commitment comes in. Dr. William Mitchell taught me about the difference between interest and commitment. It's a very interesting distinction. So, I'n applying his lesson to character—and asking: Are you simply interested in taking the road to good character...or are you committed to it?

Let's walk on down the beach and think about it for a bit. I see the shrimp boats and fishing boats anchored offshore. The seagulls are swarming over the boats in the cloud November sky. They are relentless in their pursuit of a fishy snack. The fishermen are bringing in their boats, and people are gathering to look over the catch might include

I think about the catch of the day. In our own lives, we each have a net. We can fill it wi all that is good: respect, caring, honesty, kind words and deeds, and integrity. Good character traits just don't magically appear in our nets. We have to work at getting them there...each day. We have to go fishing for them! If we are not intentional in our efforts, we can incidentally cast our nets into murky waters and come up with a less desirable catch.

Let's take a peek in the fishermen's nets. In the nets are shrimp, crabs, grouper, and a stingray. There is also lots of seaweed, a few broken shells, and an old bottle— things that get in the way of catching more fish. Unlike the fishermen, we have control over what we catch in our nets! By the thoughts we think, the words we say, the habits we maintain, and the deeds we do—we choose our catch of the day. It takes wisdom and work, but good character can be caught in our own personal nets.

Beach Chair Wisdom: Remember that a person of character allows no exceptions to doing the right thing. We, alone, have control over the character traits that we choose to become habits in our lives. Be careful o} what you choose to catch in your net. Choose to cultivate good character!

So the next time you cast your net into the sea, don't leave your catch of the day to chance. Take time to plan. Bait your hook with all that is good. Your commitment to personal growth will help you catch the traits of good character that will help make your life smoother sailing!

Soar With A
New Perspective!

t was a long-awaited beach trip. I had just gotten two and a half months of teaching
hool under my belt—and was feeling the pull of the harvest moon and the ocean. I
ok my three personal days, tied them in with Election Day, Veterans' Day, and the
o framing weekends, and…like magic, I had the nine-day beach trip of my dreams!
ff I went…smiling. It's the one time of the year that I save just for me.

his year I had a friend who was living at the beach. He's a physical therapist who
avels all over the country at thirteen-week intervals. This particular fall, he was
ationed at Litchfield Beach, South Carolina—just seven miles away from our family's
ach house. Doug and I had promised we would find some time during my visit to
lk the beach together. During the school year, Doug had been faithful about his
one calls to West Virginia. He'd call from his beachfront porch and hold the phone
t towards the ocean so I could "see" the pelicans as they flew by. Then he'd give me the
y-by-play description of life by the sea. It was a phone call that I lived for!

e phone would ring and I'd reach for the best part of my day. Over the wires and
ross the miles, his voice would come to me. I'd close my eyes and listen as his voice
inted the ocean on a canvas in my mind. With the sound of his voice I'd be off, far
ay to the south—watching the flat seaside clouds drift by his window and feeling the
ft ocean breezes blow through my hair. As we would talk, I'd hear the ocean in his
ice and beach breezes in his sighs. His call would carve a peaceful niche in the middle
my hectic life. Doug had become my eyes and ears for me, keeping me somehow
nnected to the place I love. This November, he'd actually be there. During the nine-
ur drive from West Virginia to South Carolina, I looked forward to seeing the
ach…from his perspective. I knew it would be fun.

e first evening, Doug called. "It won't be long before the full moon rises out of the
ean, Deb." That's all it took to get me going! I made the short drive to Litchfield
ach and found Doug's beach home. It was a grand house, complete with fireplace,
king chairs, and a front porch overlooking the ocean. From the porch were steps

leading up to the roof. We made the climb. There it was…a crow's nest in all of its glory, complete with built-in benches for a bird's-eye view of the ocean. Wow! I knew it was going to be a wonderful night.

I sat, stilled with wonder, as the full moon began rising out of the ocean. It was so big, so perfectly round, and so achingly beautiful. The moon passed from red through orange and yellow to white. I just sat there—covered with chill bumps—and watched. was spellbound and silent as tears welled up in my eyes. Doug could tell I was quite moved, and I believe he got a real thrill out of sharing that moon with me. It was a moment I'll always remember and cherish.

Doug went on to tell me that the tradition of carving jack-o'-lanterns came from the full harvest moon. When the harvest moon was so round and so orange, it reminded farmers of the pumpkins in their fields. And, with the face of the man in the moon showing so clearly in the full moon, it gave them the idea to carve a face in the pumpkins during the harvest. The idea for the candle inside came from the moonlight itself—the silvery lantern in the autumn night sky!

There will never be another full harvest moon I won't think of that night in the crow's nest with Doug. Looking at things from a new perspective always helps you grow. Tha night on the roof let me see my old friend, the moon, in a new light. From the time I was two years old, I have been watching the moon at night before going to sleep. Thes forty years later, Doug was able to offer me a new perspective. It was significant enoug to make this grown girl cry.

Life is like that. We grow very comfortable with ourselves—and with our attitudes, actions, and habits. We sometimes get so set in our ways we stop growing. I feel we're either growing or dying—there's no staying the same. Our character is like that, too. Are we spending life growing in good character traits, or are we comfortable staying the same? Do we need to climb the steps to the crow's nest of life and offer ourselves a new perspective?

The birds along the shore soar high in the coastal sky. Seagulls float effortlessly through the salt air; pelicans dive from higher altitudes to catch a morning snack. When I sat in the crow's nest that fall evening, I could see the ocean scenery from their perspective. It stirred me and helped me to decide I never want to get so comfortable in my own ways that I refuse to see things from a new perspective. Looking at life from a new perspective—perhaps another person's viewpoint— is a wonderful way to keep growing in character!

Beach Chair Wisdom:
Are you stuck in the ruts of life? Soar with the shorebirds! Find your own crow's nest and climb to new heights. See things from a new perspective. Is your character growing or dying? Rise to the challenge of personal growth!

Set Sail On The Sea Of Your Dreams!

1 1865 Henry David Thoreau sat in this very spot overlooking the ocean. Cape Cod ational Seashore. Nauset Lighthouse. These one hundred and thirty-three years later, m overwhelmed by it…because I am here. In this same spot. Looking out over this me sea. My dream of coming to this shore and seeing this lighthouse—is almost as old the sea itself. The realization of my dream found me lumpthroated and filled with ve. I can't remember a time in recent years when I have felt so blessed.

ew England has always pulled me. From the time I had my first pair of scissors, I have en cutting out pictures of her best scenery. Rocky coastlines, fishing villages, wooden cks, rickety sailboats, and historic lighthouses. It didn't matter where or how I got ose pictures. I just had to have them! My collection transcended the shoe box from y favorite pair of childhood sneakers. I had those pictures saved…everywhere. In fending the ruined books and magazines with missing pages, I'd always tell my mom: ve just gotta have the pictures until I can go there and see it myself!" Just give me a aside village with weathered cottages, fishing boats, and old wooden docks—any day. r me, the road to New England was the road to happiness.

l of my adult life, I had tried to go. And all of my adult life, my personal roadmap to rthern destinations seemed to get lost. Twenty years of reasons not to go made the eam of going to New England fiendishly elusive. Over the years, however, my hope of ing to New England never diminished. In fact, it intensified with time. And finally I s here. I shook my head in disbelief. I was so overwhelmed by the magnitude and citement of it all, that I just had to sit for a bit…and write. To give it time to really k in. To take in the beauty of it all. To help me savor the moment. To make sure I ptured this memory forever on paper.

e seen seven lighthouses today, smelled the fishy docks and wharves of Provincetown, d a seafood lunch, browsed a seaside row of souvenir shops, and climbed the hills that erlooked the sea. I've smiled all day long! Each experience seemed to out-do the hers. Here I sit in my old familiar beach chair in the small village of Wellfleet. The sand is at my feet, and for the first time today I'm level with the ocean. Small sand dunes separate me from the waves. A few fishing boats are anchored nearby in the cove, and one sailboat braves the wind. It's a record-setting March day in Boston—eighty-four degrees downtown and sixty degrees along the shore. Incredible for a winter's day!

I feel so at home with the squawk of the gulls and the salty breeze. It is just me and the sea again—on a northern shore. I'm not sure how I deserved to get this day. If it were my last, I would die fulfilled and happy. Some dreams are worth waiting an entire lifetime for. This was one of those dreams.

It was the trip of a lifetime. A business trip planned for the tail-end of winter ended up blossoming into a spring-like trip filled with dreams-come-true…and fun. This Boston Sunday I had gotten up early. I walked the historic streets of town. Street signs for Beacon Street and Commonwealth Avenue made me smile. I watched the *Boston Globe* delivery truck pull to the curb, as the favored newspaper was tossed to shore.

After stopping at a little out-of-the-way restaurant for breakfast, I took my to-go bag and drove over to the waterfront between Boston and Cambridge and shared my breakfast with Mother Nature. The morning was crisp and clear. Runners came to exercise in the park. The rowing team from Boston University was gliding up and down the Charles River. In perfect unison they rowed, soon joined by the rowing team from Harvard. I marveled at each stroke of the oar and at the synchronicity of their efforts. As I sat, I thought about the opportunities that we create through practice and hard work. That discipline, developed over the course of a lifetime, spills over into the other arenas of our lives. It gives us opportunities to set sail on the sea of our dreams.

I thought about my own travels. I had come to New York and Boston to study with some inspiring leaders in my field of specialty. But a Sunday escape from business let me chart my day in the direction of the Cape. All my life I had wanted to go. When the time came, I seized the opportunity and set my sails in the direction of my childhood dreams. I'm here to say that it made for grand sailing!

Beach Chair Wisdom: *Look for the many opportunities that life has to offer. Set your goals, work hard, and say yes to every opportunity that will help you reach your dreams. If opportunity doesn't knock, build a boat. Then, set sail on the sea of your dreams!*

So when it comes time for you to chart your direction in life, go back to the dreams of your childhood. Dust off your shoebox collection of dreams, and think about what it is that you really want to do. Then pack up your needed supplies for the trip. Stock your boat with the discipline of determination and perseverance. And sail on…to the sea of your dreams!

Walk The Shoreline
Of Your Mind!

he shoreline of the beach is a wonderful thing. When flying out of Los Angeles, the plane turns out over the Pacific Ocean and heads down the coastline of southern California. With Catalina Island on the right and the California coastline on the left—well, it's a beautiful view any way you look at it! While visiting the West Coast a few years ago, a friend took me for a drive up Pacific Coast Highway from Santa Monica to Santa Barbara. It was a beautifully scenic drive. My friend knows how much I love the beach—and how much I enjoy watching the sunset over the Pacific Ocean. He also knows how much I love the night sky, the stars, and the moon. It was a perfect beach evening. The salt air was warm and inviting, and the sky was a beautiful shade of blue. The sunset was truly spectacular! That big, orange sun dipped slowly in the western sky—and dropped out of sight into the sparkling blue waters of the Pacific. As we drove, the sky turned from blue…to pink…to purple. The wide beaches of Santa Monica began to fade into the rocky, curved coastline of Malibu and Pacific Palisades. There were miles and miles of rocky coastline. We arrived in Santa Barbara just as twilight was at its peak. We walked to a little out-of-the-way restaurant for dinner. I remember it as the perfect dinner. The food was great, and the conversation—even better. All during the evening, I kept pinching myself. This must be a dream! Some evenings are just too good to be true. This was one of those evenings.

After dinner, we walked the pier and settled in on a bench for some serious star-watching. The stars on Orion's Belt were there in all of their glory. They seemed so big, so bright, and so close—you could almost reach out and touch them. The sights, sounds, and smells of that night are still carved into the shoreline of my mind. Just thinking about that evening still makes me smile. On the drive home that night, the moon shone over the water along the coast. As the water rolled in to shore, it crashed on the rocks in the majestic moonlight. It was just the most magnificent sight! I was like a little kid, filled with wonder at the profound beauty of it all.

On the East Coast, there are also beautiful sights along the shore. There are the high, rocky cliffs and the harbor towns along the New England coast. And further south, there are wide stretches of beach filled with sand dunes, fences, and jetties. And keeping watch on both coasts, are historic lighthouses that are breathtakingly beautiful. Wherever you're from, you've got to admit: the coastlines of America are simply extraordinary.

Let's grab a jacket and head for the shore. A walk along the beach would do us both some good. Just look at that sky! The blues have pushed away the grey skies of morning. The flat, white clouds are hovering over the horizon as a few pelicans fly in formation towards northern destinations. The shrimp boats are escorted by flocks of seagulls who squawk away the late morning hours. The children bring their little plastic buckets to dig in the sand. The lifeguards climb to duty, as the colorful beach umbrellas begin to dot the beach. Vacationers set up chairs and spread out blankets for a day in the sun. Beach bags and coolers in hand, they come for a relaxing day at the shore.

As we walk, we see people on the balconies of highrise condominiums. They have come to the coast for a vacation. They have spent their hard-earned money renting a condominium or a luxury room in a beachfront hotel. And they have come—to see the ocean. There they are, standing on their balcony—looking out over the sea. Day after day, I see them. They stand on the balcony of life…just watching.

Some folks are inside, though. They are (can you imagine it?) watching television! With the glorious coastal scenery only steps away, they are inside—shut away from it all. I just want to shout out to everyone, "Come out and discover the beauty of the shore!" Just once, I want to throw open their shutters of isolation and let the coastal sunlight shine in where it hasn't shone in so long. I want to invite them to leave the balcony of just looking at life, to come on down to the sand—and actually start living it. After all, the sunlight traveled millions of miles to warm and brighten our life. We don't even have to meet it halfway…just a few small steps will do!

The beach is a place of great beauty and enjoyment. But you've got to make the effort to seek it out. You've got to leave the balcony! You've got to come on down to the shore. You've got to take off your shoes, and walk the sandy beach. You've got to feel the sun on your skin. You've got to feel the beach breezes blow through your hair. You've got to come out of your shell to experience what's here!

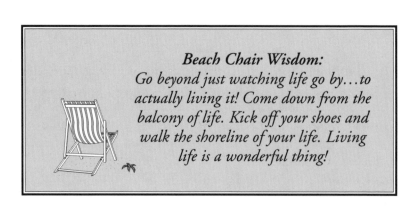

Beach Chair Wisdom:
Go beyond just watching life go by…to
actually living it! Come down from the
balcony of life. Kick off your shoes and
walk the shoreline of your life. Living
life is a wonderful thing!

Seashells Help Us Remember!

've always been a collector. During my first trip to the shore as a child, I fell in love with seashells. The less perfect they are, the better. The rough, cracked, and weathered ones are always my favorites. They've seen a lot of life—and they have survived to tell the story. I know that many people pick up seashells and put them to their ear. The legend goes that you can hear the roar of the ocean in the shell. My take on that story is a little different. I think that you can listen to seashells. But I think what you will hear is…their stories and lessons on life.

remember the first childhood shells that I ever found. I would dig and dig, with my little child-sized bucket and shovel. Those finds were like buried treasures! They always got me excited. I'd wash them off and put them out in the sun to dry. By the end of the trip, I had a nice little bag of favorites to bring home with me. To this day, I still collect shells. Over the years, I have collected many. I can still remember where I found them—and the lesson of the day. I keep shells around so that I can remember their stories.

he biggest shell I ever found was on Pawleys Island. Weeks after Hurricane Hugo blew n, the beach was still strewn with litter. While walking the beach, I noticed something ticking up out of the sand. I could tell it was something big, but figured it was storm debris. But on second thought, I backed up and stooped down for a closer look. After a little digging with my hands, I could tell that it was a shell. I tugged until it was free from the sand. It was huge! It was weathered and worn…and perfect. This conch shell had so many nooks and crannies in it. I knew it had more than one story to tell. Today m still amazed by the size and strength of that shell. When I look at it, I'm reminded of the power of that hurricane. Like the shell on the beach that day, we all have the power to weather the storms of life—and survive to tell the story. That shell will always remind me of the resilience we need for life.

nother favorite is a small brown-and-white nautilus shell I found on the beach in Cape Cod. It was the only shell I found that whole day. It's mostly smooth and swirled, and is cracked and worn in only a few places. It has had an easier life. That day on The Cape made me appreciate the good days that we have in life—the days when our sailing is over smooth waters. With that shell to remind me, I'll try not to take the good times in life for granted.

On Garden City Beach, I found the neatest little heart-shaped shell. I've had it for many years. It is a small, flat piece of a shell—that has been worn down by the sea into a distinctive heart shape. I love this shell so much that I always carry it with me. If you were to reach into the pocket of my khaki shorts, you would find it there. I carry it with me so that I can grab a beach visit wherever I happen to be. When I reach into my pocket and feel that little shell, it just takes me away!

Life's journey is like a walk on the beach. As we walk, we see shells scattered along the sand. Each shell is reminiscent of an event, a memory…a life lesson. Each day we walk the sands of time, we experience more of life. And with each experience we learn something new. Each seashell has its story. We need to take the time to listen to each shell and remember its lesson.

Over the years, seashells have added to my personal scrapbook of memories. They remind me of our family's life journey over four generations. In my collection there are shells I found as a child while playing on the beach with my grandmothers—and a shell or two my own sons found when they were playing on the beach with me. I have shells my mom and I found together on the beach—just months before she died. Life seems to come full circle. I treasure the shells that Dad shared with me after Mom's death. Many of her favorite shells are right where she left them—on the shelf in the kitchen window at our family's beach house. Whenever I'm washing dishes, it's like looking back over Mom's life, one shell at a time. I feel like she's sharing her memories and wisdom with us these many years later.

With each day's walk on life's golden sands, we learn something new. Each new experience is a wonderful teacher. So take time to pick up your own personal seashells and listen. Listen to the stories…and remember the lessons. The lessons learned yesterday and remembered today can help you deal with your experiences tomorrow!

Beach Chair Wisdom:
Seashells are wonderful souvenirs from the sands
of the past. Each shell has its own story…and lesson. These treasures
from the sea can help us remember what we've learned. On your next
beach walk, pick up the shells and listen. There's always
a lesson echoing inside!

Heaven Won't Be Such A Big Adjustment!

My brother Tom loved the beach. He had that proverbial saltwater running through his veins. He and I shared a love of the sea. Whenever we were at the beach, we always felt a little like we must be in heaven.

When we were young, our family vacations always were routed south. Virginia Beach, North Carolina's Outer Banks, and South Carolina's Grand Strand were our destinations. When we grew up, nothing changed in the vacation department. The seashore was like this giant magnet to the Austin family. We were always instinctively pulled there.

Our love for the beach brought our family closer. We didn't have to explain to one another the attraction. With just one look at the seashore, we would smile—and know that we all felt the same way. It was like being each other for just that one moment in time. The beach somehow connected us. We were all beach bums at heart, walking barefooted on the sand in our shorts and tee shirts. When we were at the beach, we were always happy. It was the Austin version of heaven on earth.

In 1985, Mom and Dad bought a place at the beach. My brother Pat had worked in Garden City Beach, South Carolina, during his college summers. At one summer's end, he was struck by a billboard message when heading for home: "Why leave the good life?" The message of that billboard really got under Pat's skin. He came right back home and transferred from West Virginia University to Coastal Carolina University. When asked by family members why he was transferring, Pat would just relay the billboard's message. It was easy to understand.

Pat lived at the beach during his college years. Whenever the rest of us could get away, we'd head for the coast, too! Over the years, we put a lot of beachbound miles on our cars' odometers. And, with every beach visit, we grew closer as a family. From West Virginia to South Carolina, we would come. Spring, summer, fall, and winter—it was the same. We were drawn to the sea. Individually and collectively, we were pulled...and mesmerized...and filled with wonder. We just couldn't get enough of life-by-the-sea.

In recent years, Tom moved away. He took his family to Texas. Tom missed his visits with the family at Garden City Beach, but would journey to the Gulf Coast to see the ocean. One of my favorite pictures of him is on that beach. One thing that was difficult for Tom was the distance between us. He longed to come home for the holidays, home for the weekend…home for no reason at all. From Texas to West Virginia is a two-day drive, and so the visits became few and far between. It was hard to be separated. But the beach was one way for our family to stay connected.

Tom and I had more than the beach in common. He, too, was a dreamer and a writer. We were kindred spirits who knew and loved the power of words. We both loved to think and to write late at night. We loved to be outside and to feel the fresh night air on our skin. We would both sit for hours—Tom in Texas and me in West Virginia— looking up into the night sky. We would look at the moon and think of each other. Somehow, the moon also kept us connected.

It was I who first fell in love with the moon. It wasn't long in life before Tom joined me. We were like the early sailors who looked to the night sky for guidance and direction. We used the stars to chart our journeys.

Tom was a sailor. The last three years were not smooth sailing for him. After Mom died in April of 1995, Tom was never the same. He grieved for her, and looked for solace in the empty promises of alcohol. He traveled over rough and unyielding seas. For many months, he struggled just to keep his head above water. Tom lost his life on the sea of alcoholism in October of 1998. He valiantly fought the storms of life and the forces of nature. At the tender age of thirty eight, he died at sea. That day was the hardest of my life. My heart was completely broken. Fortunately, he was found at sea—by the Keeper of the Stars, who took mercy on him because of his struggles and called him home. Tom is now safe and free of that wretched disease. He has sailed on to safer shores…and is now docked near Mom's Lighthouse in Heaven's Harbor. In Tom's last hours, Mom's light surely showed him the way.

Very hard days for me came after Tom's death. How to go on living became the question of each new day. I needed guidance and direction more than at any time in my life. The sky was full of clouds, and I felt I'd lost my way. I was far away from the beach, which had always made me feel centered and connected to my family, and I was grasping for answers. I needed a guiding light, a compass to get me back on track. Beach stars have always seemed bigger and brighter to me. The way that they hang in the sky over the ocean makes anything seems possible. I desperately needed now to reach for those stars. And so I planned a November beach trip.

I packed the car with my beach journal and a few clothes. Also, in a special box were some of Tom's ashes. During his last months, he had wished only for a trip to the shore. I was determined to get him there. I made arrangements to miss a few days of school and was on my way…alone. Like the early sailors, I followed the stars in the night sky and found myself home…at the beach. God's timing is always perfect. The full harvest moon was scheduled to be there. I went down to the shore to await its coming. I took my beach chair and parked it in the sand. I wrote my way through the setting of the sun in late afternoon. As I looked out over the ocean, I gave thanks for the gift of the beach in my life—and for the many lessons that I have learned at the shore. Again I listened to the earth, and I saw that it was good. The November breeze was warm and gentle, and I felt that my last minutes with my little brother were sweet and tender. Just as the sun began its decent in the evening sky, I wrote this message in the sand:

TOM AUSTIN
1960 - 1998
He loved it here.

I drew a heart in the sand, and sprinkled a few of Tom's ashes there in the heart. I watched the incoming tide wash away the message and the ashes—just as the full harvest moon rose up from the wonderful sea. It was a very touching experience. Just as that big, orange moon came up out of the water—a few dolphins, who were playing close to shore, jumped out of the water to become silhouettes framed by perfect moonlight. As the tears streamed down my face, I threw the last of Tom's ashes into the night breeze. As I did, two pelicans flew by. I recognized it as a heavenly sign: Mom had come to get Tom—and together they were flying from the coastal skies to heaven. Tom's Beach Moonrise Memorial Service was now over. My mission in his honor had been accomplished. Part of Tom had been buried at sea… that part was his heart. It seemed only right.

My time with my brother had come to an end. All that was left was the letting go. I stood on the shore alone, in the coming darkness of the autumn night. The evening stars began to dot the sky. I knew I needed to pay attention. Stars can show you the light in life when all you can feel is the darkness. The majestic harvest moonlight was sparkling on the water. The moon and stars, which had always kept me connected to Tom, were now going to be the compass that charted my new direction in life.

As I walked back to the family beach house under the light of the harvest moon, I thought about the eulogy I gave when Mom died. I took one of my own messages to heart: Friends are the stars in the night skies of life who show us the way through the darkness when we have lost our way. I knew that this message was meant for me, too. I leaned on its wisdom.

I thought back to Tom's life, and how it had been smooth sailing for so many years. Then came his entry into rough and dangerous seas. I had wanted to save him from the desperation of that journey. I will always regret that I wasn't able to save him—or give him the life raft that he needed. But like the incoming tide, his disease couldn't be stopped. We were all powerless in the effort.

As I lay in bed that night watching the moon from my window, I thought about the many lessons that I had learned from the sea. I thought, too, about the many lessons that I had learned from my little brother. From Tom, I learned to cherish life. I learned to experience the real joy in life and in nature—especially at the shore. I learned to love unconditionally, despite the risk of being hurt. I learned that goodness counts, and that being good often means being lonely. I learned that we are not always in control of our destiny.

With his life, Tom taught me to love life with all of our strength and being. And that when sailing is rough, to tie a knot on the end of our nautical rope—and to hang on. And with his death Tom taught me that, when the time comes to sail on to Heaven's Harbor, to learn to let go. The question still lingered. Why leave the good life? Tom would have left for only one reason. To go on to a better life!

I love my little brother. And I would give anything to have him back in my life. But for him, I have learned to give thanks that his voyage on the sea of alcoholism is over. He is now sailing in peace, in a better place. In fact…he's now in the best place! I have to believe that. It helps me to think that, God in His goodness, gives us each the heaven that we need. And so, I believe that Tom has found a heavenly beach to enjoy for all eternity. My brother knew and loved the beach. Because of that, heaven won't be such a big adjustment!

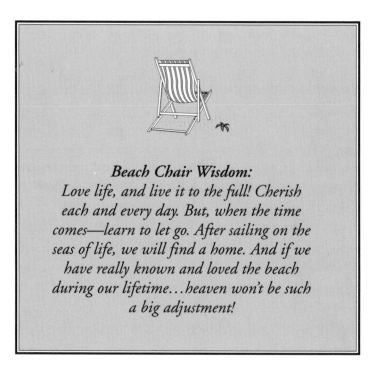

Beach Chair Wisdom:
Love life, and live it to the full! Cherish
each and every day. But, when the time
comes—learn to let go. After sailing on the
seas of life, we will find a home. And if we
have really known and loved the beach
during our lifetime…heaven won't be such
a big adjustment!

One Pelican Can Make A Difference!

Never underestimate the power of one. It's great wisdom, any way you look at it. From the rocking chair, the teacher's chair…and the beach chair, it's definitely a lesson worth learning. From my childhood I learned firsthand the power of one caring adult in the life of a child. That caring and interest goes a long way in helping a child develop a life of goodness and happiness. Whether it's a parent, grandparent, teacher, or friend—time spent with a loving, caring adult is a powerful catalyst for growth in any child's life.

I had the most wonderful childhood. I'm so grateful I grew up surrounded by people who loved me and believed in me. I had parents, grandparents, great grandparents, sisters, brothers, teachers, neighbors, and friends—all to lean on for advice and wisdom. From them, I learned many of lessons that have stayed with me throughout my life. Many times I learned my lessons the hard way—by ignoring their wisdom and by making mistakes. Lessons learned the hard way are always the most powerful because the pain and heartbreak carve them forever in our memories. We could, at those times, walk away feeling like failures. But love is a wonderful thing. People who love you and believe in you always support you, too. It makes a wonderful difference by helping to turn those little failures into big successes. We all know that there will be times in life when we experience failure. My friend Hal Urban wrote about it in his insightful book, *Life's Greatest Lessons*. Hal tells us that "it is O.K. to fail—everyone else has." He quotes General George S. Patton for emphasis: "Success is how high you bounce after you hit bottom." People who love us will help make sure that we bounce back, too!

Teachers play a powerful role in charting the destiny of a child. By taking a child under his wing, a teacher can propel a student to achieve the greatness within. A teacher's greatest charge is to believe in his students until they can come to believe in themselves. I know that to be true because I had many good teachers during my schooling. Lucky for me, I also had a few great teachers! They helped shape the course of my life in wonderful ways. I know, too, that I've been a similarly strong influence in the lives of my own students. I never take that responsibility lightly. It's a joyful moment when a parent takes the time to tell me I made a positive difference in the life of his child. Even more special is the treat of hearing the news, years later, from the student himself.

Pack up your beach gear, and let's head on down to the shore for a last seaside stroll together. It's time to learn about the power of one from one of the best teachers of all—nature. Just look at the sky! The blue sky is filled with sunshine, and the salt air is dancing through the palm trees. The water sprays the rocks as waves crash to shore. The seagulls and sandpipers tiptoe through the surf as it caresses the warm sand. And, there in the late afternoon sky is the fella I've been waiting for—my friend, the pelican. Somehow he always seems to show up just when I need him the most.

I've spent lots of my life at the beach. Since my parents bought our South Carolina beach home, I've had many opportunities to enjoy the seashore. For many of those years, I'd make several trips to the beach—spring, summer, fall, and winter. I just couldn't stay away. Sometimes I was fortunate enough to have friends who traveled with me, but many of those times I came to the beach by myself. It can be a lonely trip if you let it. The first summer that I came for an extended stay, I'll have to admit was more difficult than I thought it would be. There's only so much solitude you need in your life. But I love the adventure of the beach, and even the lack of a traveling companion will not stop my car from heading south.

It's funny, though…when I'm at the beach I rarely feel alone because I'm in such wonderful company. Nature. At times, I feel like Henry David Thoreau—just communing with the great outdoors. There is great peace and companionship in the venture. I remember times when a walk on the beach seemed like my dearest friend—and a pelican sighting was the thrill of a lifetime. It didn't even have to be lots of pelicans flying in formation to get me excited. The sight of just one pelican has the power to cheer me up and make me smile. A pelican sighting always adds joy to my day!

Now you must be thinking that to be an odd statement. But, really think about it. There are things in your life that get you excited, make you smile, and make you feel good all over. Maybe it's a hug from a child, a perfect rose in your garden, or a lunch with a friend who makes you laugh. Take a minute to think of what they are. Are you smiling yet? I actually get excited just thinking about the pelicans—and even more excited when I really see them. I'm not sure why, but there is just something about them that makes me truly happy.

So, just as one pelican can make a difference in my day—one this-is-what-I-love-the-most can make a difference for you. Take time to get to know yourself, and then treat yourself to a smile. And don't forget to spread a little coastal sunshine into the lives of others. Life was meant to be a happy experience. Let it!

Life's Greatest Lessons, by Hal Urban. Redwood City, Calif.: Great Lessons Press, 1997

__Beach Chair Wisdom:__
Never underestimate the power
of one! One caring adult, one
act of kindness, one lucky break,
one person who believes in you,
one loyal friend—or one lone
pelican. There are things in life
that bring us joy—that make a
big difference in our attitude
and our day. Like the coastal
sun, let them shine into your
life. Here's wishing you beaches
filled with whatever it is that
makes you happy!

LESSONS FRO

It's hard to end this book. My thoughts and my pencil are fighting me all the way. As soon as this book was finished, on Easter Sunday of 1999, I got in my car and headed for the beach. It was my reward for meeting my goal. It was time for a much needed change of scenery, and time to go back to the place where I'd said goodbye to my mom and brother. It was hard, but I needed to face the sea again.

While walking the beach early one morning, I saw a beautifully scripted message in the sand. *Time flies, but remember that you are the navigator!* It looked like beach chair wisdom to me. It was hard not to stop and write about it. But I walked on. And as I walked, I thought about time. It is God's greatest gift to us. So many times in life, we waste it. We take it for granted. We even kill time. That may be the greatest sin of all.

My last morning at the beach was a serene one. It was well before dawn. Morning mist covered the horizon. Blended in the palest shade of blue, it seemed as if the sea and sky were one. I saw no horizon. Just then, a lone pelican flew by, barely skimming the waves. He was headed north. I took his lead, and followed him home. As usual, I cried. It's always so hard for me to leave the sea.

Just as I turned away from the shore, the sun came up! It was the most perfectly orchestrated sunrise I'd seen—and I knew it was meant for me. This huge, orange perfect sun was the best goodbye of all. It would be enough to get me through until my next visit.

I told my friend Phil that it will be hard not to write more lessons from the beach chair. For whenever I go to the shore, I always learn something new. Life is like that. We keep living…we keep learning. It is my hope that these lessons from nature at the edge of the sea help you in your travels. They can help keep your ship on a more even keel. If you live the character message taught at the shore, you will find that life is more of a breeze! Enjoy each moment!

About the Author

Deb Brown is a teacher by heart. She has been honored with several teaching awards, including the Milken Family Foundation National Educator Award and the Ashland Oil Teacher Achievement Award. Her work extends beyond the classroom to include speaking about her books and character development at education conferences and schools across America. She has carried the character message to parents, students, and educators from thirty-three states.

Deb is the author of *Lessons From The Rocking Chair: Timeless Stories For Teaching Character*. She spends her free time writing, beachcombing, and watching the night sky. Deb lives in her hometown of St. Albans, West Virginia, in an empty nest vacated by her two sons, Aaron and Ben. She spends her summers in Garden City Beach, South Carolina.

To my parents...Margaret and Jack Austin: Thank you for passing on to me your love for the sea! It has been a most cherished part of my heritage. I will never be able to thank you enough for providing me with a home by the sea. It has been a wonderful refuge for me over the years, and has helped me return to the shore for more wisdom and guidance in life. Because of you, I was able to learn and pass on the *beach chair wisdom* in this book.

To my brother...Tom Austin: Thank you for sharing with me your love and passion for the sea. I miss you every single day, but I know that you are enjoying coastal life...in heavenly ways!

To my sisters and brother...Ellen, Stephanie, and Pat: It has been fun growing up with you on hometown streets and beachtown sands. The lightkeeper in Heaven's Harbor will forever keep us close.

To my nephews...Brian, Elliott, and Ethan: There's no escaping it! A love of the beach is a part of your heritage and inheritance. It is my hope that you continue to live and learn there for all of your life. After all, life's greatest lessons are just a beach trip away!

To my grandmothers...Nanny and Nina: Vacations with you at the beach are among my finest childhood memories. Thanks for making sure that I discovered the *real* treasure of being at the shore!

To my beach friend and mentor...Mike Mitchell: I have learned so much from you and the sea. Because of you, my beach trips have been full of fun and learning. The lessons from the shore are the greatest character lessons in nature. Thanks for giving me the opportunity to grow and learn by the sea! This book is the result of that adventure and wisdom.

To my hometown friends...Kathryn Ross, Linda Taylor, Pat Cline, Kay Lee, Ann Perkis King, Chris Ketterly, and Jane Roberts: Your friendship has continued to bring me happiness and support. Hometown friends are always the *best* friends!

To the students in my Lakewood Character Class: You taught me so much during my year with you! Because of *your* lessons on character I have grown as teacher, writer, and person. Hang on to that *moral rope* of character instruction—so that your life will be anchored in the character message. I love you all very much!

To my new friends and colleagues…at Weimer Elementary School: Your love and support for my teaching and my writing have spurred me on! Thanks for helping me share the character message in my new school.

To my Weimer Sixth Grade Students…April, Danielle, Johnny, Holden, Ashley, Zack, Casey, Sarah, Jeremy, Chris, Quentin, Sarah, April, Gabe, Shayne, Crystal, Abby, and Danielle: You have taught me so much about how kids learn and live the character message. I have taught you the character lessons that can make your life happy and good. It is my hope that you take the lessons to heart and live them each day. These lessons have the power to change your life in wonderful ways! I love each of you and want you to grow in knowledge…and grow in character.

To my character education colleagues from across the country…Phil Vincent, Hal Urban, Tom Lickona, Matt Davidson, Kevin Ryan, Ben Nesbit, Charlie Abourjilie, Helen LeGette, Jerry Corley, David Wangaard, David Brooks, Roger Phillips, Rich Parisi, Sue Cummings, and Deb McGowan: Thank you for all that you have taught me about character and life. Because we have the same life's mission of spreading the character message, you have become dear and cherished friends. I respect and applaud you…and your life's work!

To my character education colleagues on the homefront…Trish Hatfield, Barbara Walters, Doug Walters, Carol Thom, Sherrie Davis, Mickey Blackwell, and Nancy Shumate: It has been a joy to get to know you and work with you! Our weekly meetings at Fawn's Place have given me greater insight into the importance of our work. Thanks for your part in seeing the character message spread throughout our district and state.

To the professionals at Character Development Publishing…Dixon Smith, Phil Vincent, Lisa Brumback, Ginny Turner and Sandy Nordman Pogue: With sincere respect and appreciation, I thank you for making my second book a reality. As a writer and messenger of the character message, I appreciate your help in seeing the message spread. You've not only made my personal dream come true, but you have helped to make the world a better place…one book at a time!

To my sons…Aaron and Ben: The sea is one of God's best creations. Giving *you* life and wisdom was my greatest work—and joy! Now, you have moved away and are on your own. It is my deepest wish that the character lessons learned in your childhood will guide you on your own journey through life. I want to pass on, as part of your heritage, my love for the sea and the many lessons learned at the shore. I wish you a life filled with love and goodness—and the wisdom to find your way. I will always be here for you—loving you and believing in you. It is your responsibility to help make the world a better place. It is my hope that this collection of *beach chair wisdom* helps!

MORE GREAT RESOURCES

	Quantity	Price	Total
ADVISOR/ADVISEE CHARACTER EDUCATION 24 Lessons to Develop Character in Students, SARAH SADLOW		$24.95	
CHARACTER EDUCATION Superintendent's & Administrator's Guide To..., DUANE HODGIN		$3.95	
CHARACTER EDUCATION WORKBOOK A "How-To" Manual for School Boards, Administrators & Community Leaders, JUDITH HOFFMAN & ANNE LEE		$12.00	
DEVELOPING CHARACTER IN STUDENTS, 2nd Edition A Primer for Teachers, Parents & Communities, PHILIP VINCENT		$19.95	
JOURNEYS IN EDUCATION LEADERSHIP Lessons From Eighteen Principals of the Year, ALICE HART		$12.00	
LESSONS FROM THE ROCKING CHAIR Timeless Stories For Teaching Character, DEB BROWN		$8.95	
PARENTS, KIDS & CHARACTER 21 Strategies for Helping Your Children Develop Good Character, HELEN LEGETTE		$15.95	
PROMISING PRACTICES IN CHARACTER EDUCATION Nine Success Stories from Across the Country, VARIOUS		$12.00	
PROMISING PRACTICES IN CHARACTER EDUCATION, VOL. 2 12 New Success Stories from Across the Country, VARIOUS		$14.00	
RULES & PROCEDURES IN CHARACTER EDUCATION The First Step Toward School Civility, PHILIP VINCENT		$14.00	
RULES AND PROCEDURES VIDEO The First Step Toward School Civility, 44. MIN, PHILIP VINCENT		$99.95	
TEACHING CHARACTER Teacher's Idea Book, ANNE DOTSON & KAREN WISONT		$24.00	
Parent's Idea Book, ANNE DOTSON & KAREN WISONT		$12.00	

SHIPPING:
Up to $25 ....$4
$25 to $100 ....$6
Over $100 ....6%

Subtotal

NC Tax (6%)

Shipping

Form of payment: Check ☐ PO # — — — — —   Total — — — — —
Make checks payable to:
Character Development Publishing, PO Box 9211, Chapel Hill, NC 27515-9211

Ship To:
Name

Organization _____ Title

Address

City: _____ State: _____ Zip:

Phone: (__) _____ Signature:

FAX ORDERS: (919) 967-2139
For further information, or to schedule a Character Development
Workshop, call (919) 967-2110, or e-mail to Respect96@aol.com or visit
our WebSite at charactereducation.com   (Call for quantity discounts) LBC2000

CHARACTER
DEVELOPMENT
G R O U P
PO Box 9211
Chapel Hill, NC 27515

CHARACTER DEVELOPMENT GROUP offers complete resources,
including publications and staff development training for
the planning, implementation and assessment of
an effective character education program in schools and
school systems.

"*Lessons From The Beach Chair* will bring smiles to your face and tears to your eyes. You won't be able to put it down or walk away from it."

CHARLIE ABOURJILIE
Character Education Coordinator
Guilford County (N.C.) Schools

"Just as the sight of pelicans gliding effortlessly in formation down the beach is sure to warm your heart and lift your spirits, so will this new work by Deb Brown. The sea and the beach have inspired many people through the ages—let the wisdom in *Lessons From The Beach Chair* inspire you!"

MICHAEL A. MITCHELL
Executive Director
Power of Positive Students
International Foundation

"This is a book that belongs on your bedside table, in your briefcase, with your best friend, and on your bookshelf. It is beautifully written and offers beneficial lessons on living."

B. DAVID BROOKS, PH.D.
Author, Young People's Press
Lessons in Character

"In *Lessons From The Beach Chair*, Deb Brown shares two passions— her love for the sea and her commitment to the character message. This sensitive, caring teacher invites us to look beyond the obvious and find meaning and joy in simple wonders. This book—like that special shell found early in the morning—is truly a treasure."

DR. HELEN LEGETTE
Administrator Emeritus
Burlington (N.C.) City Schools